You Stay

THE ESSENTIAL FAN GUIDE TO

RuPaul's
Drag Race

JOHN DAVIS
ILLUSTRATED BY LIBBY VANDERPLOEG

Contents

The Herstory of RuPaul

"Once upon a time there was a little black boy born and raised in San Diego, California, who at 15 moved to Atlanta to study Performance Art and then went on to become the most famous supermodel in the world."

RuPaul Andre Charles was a boy who always liked to play with all of the colours from the crayon box. Affirmed by his mother from an early age that he was going to be a star, RuPaul was given his unique first name by her because "ain't another motherfucker alive with a name like that". After moving out of home to pursue a career in the entertainment industry studying at the North Atlanta School of Performing Arts in his teens, Ru soon dropped out knowing he needed to find his calling – something that would utilise his effervescent personality and incomparable charm.

A Jack-of-all-trades from the outset, RuPaul of the early 1980s led a punk rock band called Wee Wee Pole, go-go danced on bars, presented a cable access political gay talk show and hosted numerous local events as a smeared-lipstick, combat-boot-wearing, anti-establishment type of performer. Once the Atlanta scene grew tired for RuPaul, he moved to New York chasing his own star on the rise with other Atlanta nightlife notables Larry Tee and Lady Bunny. Teaming up with his hometown club family in New York, RuPaul began creating the original *Starrbooty* series, a pastiche of 1960s blaxploitation films, which were distributed in the nightclubs he performed in, before discovering that his dreams of super-stardom in the Big Apple were harder to reach than anticipated. After struggling for the best part of the 80s and his several moves from couch to couch and back across the country to live with his sister, Ru resettled in New York in 1989 determined to change up his act to become RuPaul the glamazon.

Following his crowning as the Queen of Manhattan in 1989 and a guest appearance in The B-52s music video for "Love Shack", RuPaul swiftly changed gears and began his ascendancy by signing with record label Tommy Boy and recording his debut studio album *Supermodel of the World*. The lead single "Supermodel (You Better Work)" was released in November 1992 and became a hit in the US and across Europe making RuPaul, the 6'7" man in drag, a household name. In the years following, RuPaul hosted the MTV Video Music Awards and the Brit Awards (with Sir Elton John) and released a UK #7 hit single with Sir Elton – a cover of the seventies hit "Don't Go Breaking My Heart" produced by disco legend Giorgio Moroder. Modelling contracts with makeup giant M.A.C. Cosmetics and a book release (*Lettin' It All Hang Out* in 1995) kept Ru's star on the rise throughout the mid 1990s before he began hosting his own talk show, *The RuPaul Show*, with radio hostess Michelle Visage in 1996. A melting pot of A-list celebrity interviews, live performances and even political discussions, *The RuPaul Show* ran for 100 episodes over two seasons and allowed Ru to meet and perform alongside many of his childhood idols including Cher and Diana Ross. Finishing off the decade with a guest starring role in *The Brady Bunch* remake film and a legendary duet of "It's Raining Men" with another of his idols, Martha Wash, RuPaul was about to embark on the third phase of his drag career – going underground again.

Faced with the post-9/11 Republican world at his doorstep, RuPaul made the creative and professional decision to take a break from showbiz after what was an incredibly successful run. Quietly releasing studio and remix albums as well as the odd club single between 2004 and 2008, RuPaul, the "Supermodel of the World" was faced with a lack of promotion and support from the industry that built him up only ten years prior. Armed with a new outlook on his place in the universe, RuPaul began working on a new television opportunity, inspired by the success of Tyra Banks' *America's Next Top Model*.

RuPaul's Drag Race aired its first season in 2009 on LGBT-focused lifestyle cable channel Logo TV and the rest is *her*story. Going from strength to strength over nine main cycles and two *All Stars* seasons between 2009 and 2017, *Drag Race* harnessed the revisiting of 1990s pop culture in mainstream society. Bringing together fierce drag competitors from across the US, Puerto Rico and even Australia to a gauntlet where sewing, performance, styling and comedy skills are tested to discover "America's Next Drag Superstar", RuPaul has created a whole new world of drag aspiration. Incorporation of new RuPaul dance anthems like "Glamazon", "Sissy That Walk" and "Cover Girl" into the programming allowed for new fans of his music to jump on board the train that started two decades earlier. As the popularity of the show and viewership increased from season to season, RuPaul created RuPaul's DragCon in 2015, the first ever convention focused on drag queens, their artistry and cultural impact. RuPaul, the ultimate glamazon, supermodel and all round queen bee isn't showing signs of slowing down... And neither are his girls.

RuFacts + Figures

THE MOGUL

RU-ENTERPRISE MERCHANDISE:
RuPaul Limited Edition
Collector's Figurine

"Glamazon" fragrance
by Colorevolution

RuPaul Bar (peanut butter and
sea salt chocolate bar) from Sweet!
candy store, Hollywood

Lettin' It All Hang Out (biography)

Workin' It (self help guide)

WHICH RU ARE YOU?:
RuPaul as Mrs. Cummings
(*The Brady Bunch Movie*, 1995)

RuPaul as Rachel Tensions
(*To Wong Foo, Thanks for
Everything! Julie Newmar*, 1995)

RuPaul as Starrbooty
(*Starrbooty*, 2007)

RuPaul as Tyrell Tyrelle
(*Another Gay Sequel: Gays Gone
Wild*, 2008)

RuPaul as Rudolph
(*Ugly Betty*, 2010)

RuPaul as Lionel
(*Girlboss*, 2017)

THE ALBUMS

SELECTED DISCOG-RU-PHY:
*RuPaul is Star Booty: Original Motion
Picture Soundtrack* (1986)

Supermodel of the World (1993)

Foxy Lady (1996)

Ho, Ho, Ho (1997)

RuPaul's Go-Go Box Classics (1998)

RuPaul Red Hot (2004)

*Starrbooty: Original Motion
Picture Soundtrack* (2007)

Champion (2009)

Glamazon (2011)

Born Naked (2014)

Realness (2015)

Greatest Hits (2015)

Slay Belles (2015)

Butch Queen (2016)

American (2017)

*Remember Me: Essential,
Volumes 1 & 2* (2017)

THE SINGLES

THE LOOKS

Soul Train Sister by RuPaul as seen in the B-52's music video for "Love Shack"

Confederate Flag Dress by Marlene Stewart, as seen in *To Wong Foo, Thanks for Everything! Julie Newmar*

Isis Winged Showgirl by Bob Mackie, as seen at the 1995 VH1 Fashion and Music Awards

Golden Glamazon by Zaldy, as seen in *RuPaul's Drag Race* Season 4 promo

Panther On The Runway by Zaldy, as seen in *RuPaul's Drag Race* Season 6 promo

Supermodel of the World by Zaldy, as seen in the music video for "Supermodel (You Better Work)"

SIGNATURE LOOK:
Supermodel of the World Realness

TYPE:
The Glamazon

QUE

ENS

Acid Betty

"No need to adjust your
TV sets. This acid trip is all real!"

WHAT'S THE T?

Hailing from Brooklyn, New York, Acid Betty (Jamin Ruhren) started her drag takeover in 2005 in response to her disillusion with the traditional underground drag scene. In the decade predicating her appearance on Season 8 of *Drag Race*, Acid Betty's notoriety in the New York drag scene ascended as she pushed the edges of style, makeup and hair artistry to become a legend of the alternative drag scene. Work with Cazwell and an appearance on *Project Runway* brought Acid Betty's artistry to the public eye but her appearance on *Drag Race* opened the world up to the out-of-this-world genius with killer punk and alien-esque looks slaying the main stage.

QUICK STATS

DRAG RACE: Season 8
RANKING: 8th place
SIGNATURE LOOK: Extraterrestrial Hair Extravaganza Realness
TYPE: Hybrid Drag Queen
FAN-FAVOURITE PERFORMANCE: "Ruthless Lover" by Acid Betty

Drag term

BAR QUEEN

A drag queen who makes an effort to get-up in drag but may not be one of the performers on stage – or necessarily even want to be a showgirl. Instead, she spends a lot of her time at the bar being a social butterfly. Tatianna was referred to as a "bar queen" by Shannel in Season 1 of *All Stars*, suggesting that she was hardly in the same league as the other drag queens that season.

Adore Delano

WHAT'S THE T?

A seasoned reality TV competitor, Danny Noriega made it as far as the semi finals on the seventh season of *American Idol* in 2008 before unleashing persona Adore Delano, his YouTube drag character, in 2009. Adore was the perfect blend of Noriega's fiery pop rock sensibility and his mother's so-called "ex-chola" attitude. In the lead-up to her appearance on *RuPaul's Drag Race* in 2014 Adore, inspired by hostess and *Drag Race* royalty Raven, competed and won her first drag contest at Micky's in West Hollywood in 2011.

Competing in the *Race* was a challenge for the green Delano, who fought hard to shake off the criticisms of her sloppy performance and aesthetic. She triumphed in "Shade: The Rusical" and the "Oh No She Betta Don't" rap challenge as well as in the fragrance advertisement challenge alongside drag sister Laganja Estranja, harnessing her personality and charm to forward her way into the top three of the contest. Although finishing as a co-runner up with Courtney Act, Adore won the hearts of the *Drag Race* audience and took control of the second phase of her plan to take over the world.

Releasing her debut album *Till Death Do Us Party* soon after the conclusion of Season 6, Adore Delano went on tour to promote the album across the world. Truly a cross-over star, Delano's album charted higher than any other contestant's releases on the American charts and she has created numerous music videos for the singles, including "I Look Fuckin' Cool" starring Alaska and Nina Flowers. In 2016 Adore competed as a fan-favourite in the second season of *All Stars* where her aesthetic was once again criticised by Michelle Visage, resulting in her decision to tap out of the competition in its second week.

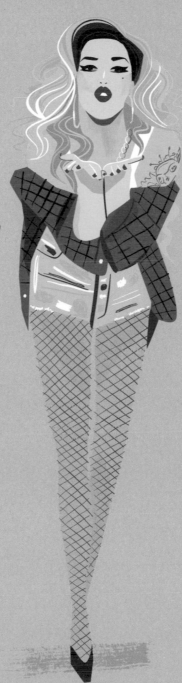

"I'm not polished enough? I'm polish remover, bitch!"

QUICK STATS

DRAG RACE:
Season 6 | *All Stars 2*

RANKING:
Co-runner Up | 9th place

POST DRAG RACE:
Released albums *Till Death Do Us Party* (charted at #59 on the US *Billboard* 200 chart) and *After Party*; starred in Starbucks' first LGBT advertisement with Bianca Del Rio

SIGNATURE LOOK:
Band T-shirt and Combat Boots Realness

TYPE:
The Diamond in the Rough

FAN-FAVOURITE PERFORMANCE:
"Patron Tequila" by Paradiso Girls

Aja

"You're perfect, you're beautiful, you look like Linda Evangelista..."

WHAT'S THE T?

A young Brooklyn legend in the making, Aja (Jan Rivera) began playing with drag at the age of 16 inspired by the big city around her and the strong imagery of anime girls and super villains. A fan-favourite from the outset, Aja's personal development in her short run on Season 9 of *Drag Race* was as exciting to watch as her always head-turning runway presentations. Continuing to build her brand and her "Haus of Aja" drag collective back in New York City, Aja is one to watch for years to come.

QUICK STATS

DRAG RACE: Season 9
RANKING: 9th place
SIGNATURE LOOK: Urban Female Alien Warrior Realness
TYPE: The Anime Queen
FAN-FAVOURITE PERFORMANCE: "Glass & Patron" by FKA Twigs

Akashia

"Every competition needs a bitch, and
that bitch is ME and I'm happy with that."

WHAT'S THE T?

Inspired by the *Queen of the Damned* film, Akashia (Eric Flint) from Cleveland,
Ohio, ascended from local performances to drag fame after appearing on
Season 1 of *Drag Race*, flaunting her sass and her ass as one of the very first
"body queens" on the show. Famous for both her slip on the main stage
and her epic lip-sync against Tammie Brown to Michelle Williams' "We Break
The Dawn", Akashia continues to entertain in nightclubs across the United
States, leaving the crowds always wanting more.

QUICK STATS

DRAG RACE: Season 1
RANKING: 7th place
SIGNATURE LOOK: Sassy Streetwalker Realness
TYPE: Sickening Stripper Queen
FAN-FAVOURITE PERFORMANCE: "Bring Me Back To Life" by Evanescence

QUICK STATS

DRAG RACE:
Season 5 | *All Stars 2*

RANKING:
Co-runner Up | Winner

POST DRAG RACE:
Stars in World of Wonder
produced web series *Bro'Laska*
with her brother Cory Binney;
Released albums *Anus* (2015)
and *Poundcake* (2016); Created
and released her very own Little
Poundcake talking doll!

SIGNATURE LOOK:
Tacky Blonde Bombshell Realness

TYPE:
The Trash to Treasure Queen

**FAN-FAVOURITE
PERFORMANCE:**
"Hieeee" by Alaska

"Hieeeeeee!"

Alaska

WHAT'S THE T?

Alaska Thunderfuck 5000 (Justin Honard) cut his teeth as a drag queen in 2009 at Fubar in West Hollywood after a departure from acting. Hailing from Pittsburgh, Alaska returned to her hometown in 2010 to pursue both a drag career and relationship with Sharon Needles with whom she formed the band Haus of Haunt. Inspired by "tranimal" and other non-conformist styles of drag, Alaska was the perfect blend of trash and glamour and drew the attention of fans for many years prior to her appearance on *Drag Race*.

Following the win of then-partner Sharon Needles, Alaska powered through Season 5 notoriously never having to lip-sync for her life just like Season 2 winner Tyra Sanchez. Winning the "Sugar Ball" and "Scent of a Drag Queen" challenges late in the contest solidified Thunderfuck's brand of trash-glamour as well as her raunchy sense of humour that garnered wide adoration from viewers of the competition; fans were tickled pink by her "Red for Filth". Although she came co-runner up with Florida powerhouse Roxxxy Andrews to Jinkx Monsoon, Alaska was able to shake off the label of "Sharon's Boyfriend" and began the road to becoming what Willam has described as "The Future of Drag".

Following Season 5, Alaska appeared on stage in *The Rocky Horror Show*, *Sex and the City* and her own show *Red for Filth* before becoming a fully fledged drag recording artist. A solo act with a string of YouTube hits, it was after being cast as a spokesmodel in a 2014 American Apparel campaign that Alaska joined forced with her fellow "AAA Girls" Willam and Courtney Act to embark on a musical direction and release their drag girl-group debut record in 2017.

Alaska was called back to compete in the second season of *All Stars* in 2016, where she proved through winning four main challenges and performing epic lip-syncs for her legacy, that she deserved her place in the Drag Race Hall of Fame alongside *All Stars* Season 1 winner Chad Michaels.

Drag term

BEAT

A queen's beat is the makeup and lashes that
are applied to create the glamazon illusion.
A truly "beat face" is a face of makeup
that is so strong that the queen would be
considered stunning or "beat for the gods"
(see also: "For The Gods"). The term can also
be used as a way to describe the process
of making over the face. For example:
"Valentina beat her face real good tonight!"

Alexis Mateo

"BAM!"

WHAT'S THE T?

A seasoned pageant queen direct from Puerto Rico via Florida, Alexis Mateo (Alexis Mateo Pacheco) has been crowned numerous titles including Miss Florida US of A and All American Goddess since commencing her drag career in 2001. After successfully reaching the top three in Season 3 of *Drag Race*, famously winning the military P.S.A. challenge, Alexis went on to compete alongside fellow Puerto Rican goddess Yara Sofia in the first *All Stars* season, where she took the catchphrases, laughs and wacky hair extravaganzas audiences love about her and turned it up to 100!

QUICK STATS

DRAG RACE: Season 3 | *All Stars* 1
RANKING: 3rd place | 6th place
SIGNATURE LOOK: Latina Princess Realness
TYPE: Puerto Rican Pageant Queen
FAN-FAVOURITE PERFORMANCE: "A Woman's Drag (Joelapuss Remix)"
by Various

Alexis Michelle

"If I see something, I say something..."

WHAT'S THE T?

A drag pro of over 15 years and lover of all things musical theatre, New York's Alexis Michelle (Alex Michaels) had won fans all over the world wide web with her So You Think You Can Drag? competition winning performances before appearing on Season 9 of *Drag Race*. Having auditioned eight times prior to her casting, Alexis entered the race as an all-singing all-swinging kinda queen with a strong performing bone and a super polished mug. While Alexis' runway presentations didn't always win the judge's applause – Lady Gaga did love her Versace inspired gown! – she delivered show stealing performances in "Kardashian: The Musical" as Kris Jenner and in the "Snatch Game", where she took the challenge win for her impersonation as Liza Minnelli. Faced with the challenge of serving three fashion-forward runway looks in the "Gayest Ball Ever" Alexis stumbled with her Village People Eleganza Extravaganza and was sent packing by to the tune of "Macho Man" by Peppermint. Following her time on Season 9, Alexis has started touring the US and released a bitch house track with fellow Racers Aja, Peppermint and Sasha Velour entitled "C.L.A.T." – celebrating New York City's queens of Club, Legend, Art and Theatre.

QUICK STATS

DRAG RACE: Season 9
RANKING: 5th place
SIGNATURE LOOK: Curve, Swerve & Cinch Realness
TYPE: The Theatre Queen
FAN-FAVOURITE PERFORMANCE: "Into The Woods/Gorgeous Medley" by Various

Alisa Summers

"I'm definitely a fishy queen.
I can walk down the street and
I can never get clocked!"

WHAT'S THE T?

Coming from a strong Florida drag family background and wins in the pageant scene, Alisa Summers (Alex Hernandez) competed in Season 4 of *Drag Race* with a solid background in the performance scene. After failing to create a memorable post-apocalyptic couture look on the runway, Alisa (and her breast plate) lost in a lip-sync battle against Jiggly Caliente (and her baked potato couture). Since her time on *Drag Race*, Alisa Summers has continued to strut her stuff on stage in Tampa, Florida, to clamouring fans.

QUICK STATS

DRAG RACE: Season 4
RANKING: 13th place
SIGNATURE LOOK: Futuristic Fantasy Fish Realness
TYPE: Sequined Show Queen
FAN-FAVOURITE PERFORMANCE: "Finally" by CeCe Peniston

Alyssa Edwards

WHAT'S THE T?

A long-time competitor in the drag pageantry circuit, Alyssa Edwards (Justin Johnson) competed and won numerous pageant titles including Miss Gay Texas America 2004–2005, Miss Gay USofA 2006 and All American Goddess 2010. A dancing queen and fierce performer from Mesquite, Texas, Alyssa appeared in the 2008 documentary *Pageant* and built her Beyond Belief Dance Company prior to her appearance on *RuPaul's Drag Race*.

Emerging as one of the most well-rounded performance queens in *Drag Race* herstory, Alyssa Edwards was immediately positioned as the nemesis of fellow contest Coco Montrese with whom they shared the history of pageant dethroning and title stripping. The history of these two contestants reared its head throughout Season 5, culminating in an epic Lip-sync for Your Life to Paula Abdul's "Cold Hearted Snake" where Edwards was ultimately out-performed by her pageant sister. Prior to her elimination Alyssa became one hell of a quotable queen, melding her southern charm with old school catchphrases to create memorable lines such as "Backrolls!?", "Get a grip, get a life and get over it" and "I don't get cute, I get drop dead gorgeous".

Winning a new legion of fans from the show, Alyssa has gone on to star in her own web series *Alyssa's Secret* where she talks about a range of topics from wigs and nails to dating in drag.

As a fashionista, Edwards has graced the LA Fashion Week Marco Marco runway on multiple occaisions. In 2016, Alyssa returned to prime time television, guns blazing, with her appearance on *All Stars* 2 where she went on to win two main challenges and solidify her status as a legendary icon of the *Race*.

"Every woman has a secret. Mine happens to be a little bigger."

QUICK STATS

DRAG RACE:
Season 5 | *All Stars* 2

RANKING:
6th place | 5th place

POST-DRAG RACE:
Stars in her very own World of Wonder web series *Alyssa's Secret*; continues to direct her Texas-based dance company Beyond Belief; choreographed and performed with pop star Miley Cyrus at the 2015 MTV Video Music Awards

SIGNATURE LOOK:
Miss America Realness

TYPE:
The Dancing Queen

FAN-FAVOURITE PERFORMANCE:
"Indestructible Medley" by Various Artists

April Carrión

"Ay Dios Mio!"

WHAT'S THE T?

Excelling as an arts college student, Puerto Rico's April Carrión (Jason Carrión) joined the Season 6 cast of *Drag Race* inspired by both the glamour and androgyny of previous contestant Nina Flowers. Following her time on the *Race* where she served colourful and creative costumes on the runway, April has continued performing and modelling in drag and has also gone on to produce the documentary *Mala Mala*, which explored the lives of drag queens and young transgender people in Puerto Rico.

QUICK STATS

DRAG RACE: Season 6
RANKING: 11th place
SIGNATURE LOOK: April Showers Realness
TYPE: Art-School Androgyny Queen
FAN-FAVOURITE PERFORMANCE: "Slow" by Kylie Minogue

Drag term

BOOGER

A drag queen who is considered inept or lazy in their drag artistry. Booger drag can also describe an aesthetic style pertaining to poorly chosen outfits, bad makeup application or sloppy performance on stage.

QUICK STATS

DRAG RACE:
Season 1

RANKING:
Winner

POST DRAG RACE:
Released several dance singles on iTunes including "I'm the Shit" (2009), "Cameroon" (2010) and "Face" (2014); Fierce Drag Professor at *RuPaul's Drag U*; makes appearances across the United States as a public speaker on pride, drag and the affect of her West African upbringing

SIGNATURE LOOK:
African Animal Skin Realness

TYPE:
The Cameroonian Goddess

FAN-FAVOURITE PERFORMANCE:
"Miss USofA 2005 Medley" by Various Artists

"Face.
Face. Face.
I give face,
beauty, face."

BeBe Zahara Benet

WHAT'S THE T?

Hailing from Cameroon, Nea Marshall Kudi Ngwa worked as a male model in Paris and had his first taste of drag after filling in for an unexpected no-show of a female model. BeBe Zahara Benet was born out of the gender-bending runway moment. She saw herself as a "strong and cunty character illusion created for entertainment and the artistic expression of the feminine psyche".

Emerging from the Minneapolis drag scene, BeBe starred in the very first season of *RuPaul's Drag Race*, bringing a sense of international influence and worldly aesthetic to the competition. Winning two main challenges, she was one of the strongest competitors only having to lip-sync for her life in a wig-throwing showdown against Ongina to Britney Spears' "Stronger". Always poised, softly spoken and serving face, BeBe Zahara Benet snatched the crown from runners up Nina Flowers and Rebecca Glasscock after an iconic appearance in the first *Drag Race* music video for "Cover Girl".

After her triumphant win in the first season of *Drag Race* BeBe went on to create a theatre piece called *Queendom* where she incorporated live original music that fused pop music with African rhythms, elaborate costuming, live singers and dance elements. In addition to her regular club spots, BeBe chose to take on the challenge of public speaking at American universities discussing how her West African upbringing balances with her drag persona and life as a gay man.

Drag term

BUSTED

Similar to "booger", "busted" is a
way to describe a queen as either
very ugly or poorly put together.

Drag term

CHEESECAKE

A term to describe a queen with not only a gorgeous and curvy body, but the ability to sell her sexiness as well. This was one of DiDa Ritz's favourite sayings as she entered the work room in Season 4.

BenDeLaCreme

WHAT'S THE T?

While pursuing a Bachelor of Fine Arts at the Arts Institute of Chicago, the now Seattle-based Benjamin Putnam started his drag career in 2002 as BenDeLaCreme. A terminally delightful drag queen housewife, DeLa's inherently political show sensibility reflected her upbringing within the drag king scene of Chicago. Following her move to Seattle, she ran DeLouRue Presents, a theatrical production company producing work featuring both drag and burlesque acts, notably Season 5 winner Jinkx Monsoon. Prior to her appearance on *Drag Race* DeLa also appeared on screen in documentary film *Waxie Moon* by Wes Hurley.

Miss Congeniality of Season 6 of *RuPaul's Drag Race*, BenDeLaCreme demonstrated exceptional sewing, comedic, musical and impersonation skills throughout the contest. Although winner of the fan-favourite "Snatch Game" portraying actress Maggie Smith in her role from *Downton Abbey*, DeLa fought off stiff critique from the judges that she hid behind character facades. In a *Drag Race* first, BenDeLaCreme lip-synced for her life on two separate controversial occasions against Darienne Lake, ultimately missing out on making the top four of the contest.

Following her season of *Drag Race*, DeLa has continued to produce shows with DeLouRue including *Freedom Fantasia* the "liberty-encrusted, justice-soaked, apple-pie-scented pageant of patriotism". In conjunction with Atomic Cosmetics she has also curated her own line of cosmetics and fragrance.

"DeLa for short.
De for shorter.
Ms Creme
if you're nasty."

QUICK STATS

DRAG RACE:
Season 6

RANKING:
5th place (Miss Congeniality)

POST DRAG RACE:
Performed in a reimagining of
Hocus Pocus with San Francisco
drag legend Peaches Christ and
Jinkx Monsoon; curated her own
line of cruelty-free cosmetics and
fragrance ("Candy from a Baby")
with Atomic Cosmetics

SIGNATURE LOOK:
Kitsch Housewife
Realness

TYPE:
The Character
Queen

**FAN-FAVOURITE
PERFORMANCE:**
"The Little Mermaid Medley"
from *The Little Mermaid
Original Soundtrack*

with
HAIR,
HEELS
and
ATTITUDE
HONEY,
I am through the roof

Drag term

COME THROUGH

An acclamation showing congratulations of effort or performance. This phrase was famously called out in Season 7 by Violet Chachki following Katya and Kennedy Davenport's lip-sync to 'Roar'.

Drag term

COOKING

To leave makeup sitting on the face for a long period of time so your own body heat melts the makeup into the skin, leaving more pigmented coverage to blend with later.

"My style is very Joan Crawford/ Bozo the Clown. It's versatile... I'm not, but the look is."

QUICK STATS

DRAG RACE:
Season 6

RANKING:
Winner

POST DRAG RACE:
Starred in the crowdfunded comedy film *Hurricane Bianca*; toured her comedy show *Rolodex of Hate* internationally from 2014 through to 2016; performed at the 2015 Vienna Life Ball alongside Courtney Act and Eurovision's Conchita Wurst

SIGNATURE LOOK:
Old Hollywood Meets Clown Realness

TYPE:
The Stand Up Comedian

FAN-FAVOURITE PERFORMANCE:
"Palladio" by Escala aka "Bianca Del Rio Makes a Dress on Stage"

Bianca Del Rio

WHAT'S THE T?

Hailing from Gretna, Louisiana, Roy Haylock started his drag artistry in 1996 after working for many years as a costume designer. Emerging as Bianca Del Rio, the sharp-tongued New Orleans Gay Entertainer of the Year performed regularly before moving to New York after Hurricane Katrina. Prior to appearing on *Drag Race*, Del Rio established herself as one of the most iconic drag performers in the US alongside other icons Linda Simpson, Lady Bunny, Sherry Vine and Hedda Lettuce. The latter three were featured alongside Bianca in the web series *Queens of Drag: NYC* in 2010 who also performed in the comedy special *One Night Stand Up: Dragtastic! NYC* on Logo TV.

After pressure from her peers and her own drive to "show 'em how it's done", Bianca Del Rio was cast in *RuPaul's Drag Race*. The immediate front runner and fan-favourite for her quick wit, strong performance in all aspects of the competition and "mama bear" disposition, Del Rio won three main challenges before taking out the crown of America's Next Drag Superstar.

Fan's unwavering support for Bianca's stinging sense of humour saw her debut film project *Hurricane Bianca* gain successful crowd-funding and was released in 2016, starring *Drag Race* alumni Joslyn Fox, Willam, Shangela and Alyssa Edwards. In the years after *Drag Race*, Bianca has successfully toured her comedy shows *Rolodex of Hate* and *Not Today Satan* spreading her brand of poison-tongued hilarity across the world.

Drag term

DUSTED

The opposite of "busted", "dusted" describes a queen who appears flawless and polished in their drag transformation. Chad Michaels is often referred to as "Mother Dust" suggesting Chad is not only professional and polished, but a drag queen to look up to for inspiration.

Bob the Drag Queen

"Purse first! Purse first! Walk into the room purse first!"

WHAT'S THE T?

Inspired by the first season of *Drag Race*, Bob The Drag Queen (Christopher Caldwell) honed her skills in New York City as a quick witted and politically aware stand-up queen of comedy for over several years before being cast on *RuPaul's Drag Race*. Excelling in costume creation challenges and bringing out two fully realised polar opposite "Snatch Game" characters (Uzo Aduba and Carol Channing), Bob harnessed her confidence and cheeky honesty to win over audiences and RuPaul to be crowned the eighth winner of the *Race*. Bob's iconic "purse first" entrance onto the main stage has lead to a successful club single of the same name and a social media meme explosion.

QUICK STATS

DRAG RACE: Season 8
RANKING: Winner
SIGNATURE LOOK: Banjee Glam Realness
TYPE: The People's Queen
FAN-FAVOURITE PERFORMANCE: "Crazy" by Gnarls Barkley

Carmen Carrera

WHAT'S THE T?

Starting her drag career in the mid 2000s, New Jersey's Carmen Carrera started performing at legendary Latino showgirl club Escuelita in the heart of Manhattan. Though many years prior to her transition into the beautiful transgender woman she is today, Carrera dealt with her sexuality and understanding of gender through honing her craft as a burlesque drag performer with the support of trans drag mother Angela Carrera. Improving her sex kitten act over the years, Carmen increased her bookings and went on to play The Polo Club in Hartford, meeting *Drag Race* alumni Manila Luzon and Sahara Davenport along the way.

Carrera was cast in the third season of *RuPaul's Drag Race* and although appearing as Christopher Roman out of drag, she became very well known for her perfect proportions and buxom booty, as critiqued by Jersey girl Michelle Visage as a crutch – "Stop relying on that body!". Though wowing audiences with countless almost-nude runway presentations, Carmen – a member of the Heathers clique – didn't win any major challenges and was eliminated twice after being brought back by the judges for a second chance at the crown.

Carrera commenced her transition soon after taping *Drag Race* in 2010. Her flawless looks drew the eye of renowned fashion photographer Steven Meisel, who had Carmen star in his "Showgirl" *W* magazine and video shoot. Although touring her burlesque drag act less frequently, Carrera has become a trans role model starring, on occasion with television star Laverne Cox, in various reality programs addressing transphobia in the wider community.

"If you find a flaw,
let me know."

QUICK STATS

DRAG RACE:
Season 3

RANKING:
6th place

POST DRAG RACE:
Featured on the fifth anniversary
cover of C*NDY magazine
along with 13 other transgender
women including Laverne Cox
and Janet Mock; poster girl for
the 2014 Life Ball in Vienna shot
by David LaChapelle; Starred
in "Showgirl" – a Steven Meisel
W magazine shoot and promo
video; petitioned to serve as a
2013 Victoria's Secret Fashion
Show model

SIGNATURE LOOK:
Bulletproof Body Realness

TYPE:
The Jersey Showgirl

FAN-FAVOURITE
PERFORMANCE:
"I Am the Body Beautiful"
by Salt-N-Pepa

Drag term

T / TEA / TEE

The T, also spelled Tea or Tee, refers to the "truth" in terms of gossip, news, information or true facts – "What's the t?" ("What's up?"). Often predicating or following a commentary or a "read" are the phrases "No tea, no shade" (i.e. "I don't mean to disrespect you.") or "All tea, all shade" (meaning: "I don't care if this offends you"). For example: "No tea, no shade – but plastic surgery wouldn't be the worst thing to happen to you."

Drag term

FISHY

A term to describe a queen's ability to appear exceptionally feminine when in drag, irrespective of how little or much makeup is used to create the gender illusion. The term refers to the colloquial likening of the scent of a woman's genitals to that of actual fish. While considered its own form of drag presentation, queens described as "fish" on *RuPaul's Drag Race* are often asked by the judges to not "rest on pretty" or rely on their body to succeed in the competition. See: Courtney Act, Farrah Moan, Kenya Michaels, Rebecca Glasscock, Carmen Carrera.

"Everything I've gone through has been because of Cher."

QUICK STATS

DRAG RACES:
Season 4 | *All Stars* 1

RANKINGS:
Co-runner Up | Winner

POST DRAG RACE:
Starred in CW's *Jane the Virgin*;
opened for Cher at the launch
of her "Woman's World" single;
Released single "Tragic Girl"
(2013) with Liquid360

SIGNATURE LOOK:
Polished Drag Mother Realness

TYPE:
The Drag Assassin

**FAN-FAVOURITE
PERFORMANCE:**
"EOY (Entertainer
of the Year) 2010
Medley" by Cher

Chad Michaels

WHAT'S THE T?

With over 20 years of experience as a drag performer, Chad Michaels is the definition of an All Star and an icon – much like her own idol Cher. Drag daughter to the legendary Hunter, Michaels hails from San Diego and has performed as one of, if not *the* premiere, Cher impersonators in the world. Impersonation of the original diva has seen Chad entertain clubs across the US to Las Vegas stages and has given her the opportunity to perform for industry favourites such as Elton John, Christina Aguilera and Cher herself.

Entering the fourth season of the *Race* as a seasoned professional, Chad Michaels was not only miles ahead of her competition in her understanding and execution of her drag skills but she set the bar for characterisation and polish. Although winning the "Snatch Game" as Cher and giving memorable performances throughout the season Chad finished as co-runner up with Phi Phi O'Hara. Chad's loss of the crown didn't last long as she was soon snatched up to compete in the first season of *All Stars* in which she took the crown and the first position in the *RuPaul's Drag Race* Hall of Fame.

Following her performance in both Season 4 and *All Stars*, Chad Michaels continues to produce and perform in the *Dreamgirls Revue*, sharing the stage with, among others, Delta Work, Jasmine Masters and her drag daughter Morgan McMichaels. A master of impersonation, Chad constantly reinvents her drag and her repertoire of characters with old-school diva Bette Davis and new-school icon Lady Gaga.

Charlie Hides

"Hi, hi, hi! It's about to get shady up in here."

WHAT'S THE T?

A cabaret and cruise liner performer for over 20 years, Boston-via-London's Charlie Hides truly is the godmother of drag and a master of shady impersonation. Through widely popular celebrity impersonation and parody videos on YouTube, Charlie entered *RuPaul's Drag Race* as a fan-favourite with audiences at the ready for her cutting sense of humour and wit – and, of course, that iconic Madonna impersonation in the "Snatch Game". Unfortunately Charlie Hides' run in the *Race* didn't last long as a stumble in the "Good Morning Bitches" challenge combined with a less than mobile lip-sync to Britney Spears' "I Wanna Go" saw "The Dame" go... home.

QUICK STATS

DRAG RACE: Season 9
RANKING: 12th place
SIGNATURE LOOK: Pop-Art Mod Realness
TYPE: The Transatlantic Dame
FAN-FAVOURITE PERFORMANCE: "Burlesque Medley" by Cher

Chi Chi DeVayne

"I don't get ready – I stay ready!" *finger snap*

WHAT'S THE T?

The lovable and self proclaimed "cheap queen" of Louisiana, Chi Chi DeVayne (Zavion Davenport) started her career much like many other queens with a spur of the moment Halloween dress up... as Nicki Minaj, of course! After years of dancing the house down in the Louisiana drag scene, the high-energy DeVayne was cast in the eighth season of *Drag Race*. Chi Chi's performance in the challenges saw her glide through the competition via an EPIC lip-sync for her life to Jennifer Holliday's "And I Am Telling You I'm Not Going" (in full black and white drag!) to the final episode and a top 4 placing. DeVayne is now following her dreams of serving powerful dance-based drag performance across the globe, slaying the children one city at a time!

QUICK STATS

DRAG RACE: Season 8
RANKING: 4th place
SIGNATURE LOOK: Southern Belle Realness
TYPE: Crafty Country Queen
FAN-FAVOURITE PERFORMANCE: "Emotions" by Mariah Carey

Coco Montrese

"Orange you glad to see me?"

WHAT'S THE T?

An icon of the drag pageantry circuit, a former Miss Gay America and Las Vegas legend Coco Montrese (Martin Cooper) has entertained legions of fans since 1992 not only as Coco but as the world's premier Janet Jackson impersonator. With pageant titles and an incomparable lip-syncing ability under her belt, Coco Montrese appeared on the fifth season of *RuPaul's Drag Race* as a contestant-to-beat. Pitted against pageant peer Alyssa Edwards (long story – just watch Season 5!) from the outset, Coco proved through three lip-syncs for her life and her win of the "RuPaul Roast" that she is strongest on stage entertaining the masses. In the years after her appearance on *Drag Race* Coco's one-liners and iconic "Tang" highlight have served as fan-favourite memes leading to her return to screens on the second season of *All Stars* where she was eliminated in the first week of the contest.

QUICK STATS

DRAG RACE: Season 5 | *All Stars* 2
RANKING: 5th place | 10th place
SIGNATURE LOOK: Janet Jackson Realness
TYPE: The Lip-sync Diva of Las Vegas
FAN-FAVOURITE PERFORMANCE: "Super Bowl Medley" by Janet Jackson

Drag term

FLAZÉDA

A mishmash of "blasé" and "laissez-faire", this term was coined by Pearl in Season 7 to convey nonchalance and being relaxed, yet in total control.

Courtney Act

WHAT'S THE T?

Emerging on Australian screens as both Shane Jenek and Courtney Act on the first season of *Australian Idol*, Courtney demonstrated her brand of fiery performance and camp sensibility enabling her to make it through to the Wild Card heat of the contest. Act immediately drew the attention of audiences, performing at the Sydney Opera House as part of the finale and touring Australia. Following the release of debut single "Rub Me Wrong" Courtney became a mainstay on morning television as a featured cosmetics spokesmodel. A big fish in a little pond, Act moved to the US in the early 2010s and became a West Hollywood karaoke hostess and YouTube star.

Courtney was cast in *Drag Race* and was soon seen as a contender for the crown. Despite a rocky reception from judge Michelle Visage who accused Act of "relying on pretty", Courtney delivered countless sickening runway presentations including her take on RuPaul in the iconic Bob Mackie silver gown. Building a friendship with on-screen star Chaz Bono as well as fellow contestants Darienne Lake, Adore Delano and Bianca Del Rio, Act came out as a co-runner up winning the adoration of new fans across the US.

After her appearance on *Drag Race*, Act became the first drag artist to perform with the San Francisco Symphony Orchestra in a performance with Cheyenne Jackson. Although she had released pop singles since as early as 2004 in Australia, in 2015 Courtney released her debut EP *Kaleidoscope* and teamed up with her fellow American Apparel Ad girls Willam and Alaska to release a string of cheeky parody singles and even their own album of original and parody material!

"If everyone else is relying on ugly, why can't I rely on pretty?"

QUICK STATS

Season 6

Co-runner Up

Became the inaugural Sydney Gay and Lesbian Mardi Gras Official Ambassador in 2015; Stars in web series *American Act* for Australian media website Junkee as a comedic US foreign correspondent; Headlined the 2017 Dragapalooza tour alongside *Drag Race* live singers like Derek Barry, Trixie Mattel and Mimi Imfurst

Catalogue Model Realness

The Fishy Queen

"Nutbush City Limits (with Jake Shears at Sydney Mardi Gras)" by Ike and Tina Turner

Drag term

THROWING SHADE

The act of subtly and wittily insulting someone; an underhand comment or backhanded compliment; bitchiness personified. Throwing shade is something the drag community have been doing for years, and so have you – you just didn't know it had a name. Here's some shade you might like to throw: "You're so confident. I just love how you don't even care what you look like."

Cynthia Lee Fontaine

"How you doin' mis amores? Are you ready to see my cucu, AGAIN?"

WHAT'S THE T?

Puerto Rico's Cynthia Lee Fontaine (Carlos Hernandez) enjoyed a successful drag career in Austin, Texas, earning titles such as Miss Texas Continental in 2012 before being cast in Season 8 of *Drag Race*. A fan-favourite despite a short run in the season, Cynthia won audiences over with both her "cucu" and her huge heart to win the title of Miss Congeniality. Amid bringing her brand of effervescent Latina *loca* to the world, Cynthia Lee Fontaine was diagnosed with stage one liver cancer, slowing down her entertainment schedule. With this in mind, RuPaul decided to give "Miss Cucugeniality" a second chance to prove herself once recovered, in the ninth season of the *Race* where she brought back the bonkers sense of humour right up until her performance as Sofia Vergara in the "Snatch Game".

QUICK STATS

DRAG RACE: Season 8 | Season 9
RANKING: 10th place (Miss Congeniality) | 10th place
SIGNATURE LOOK: Glamour Clown Realness
TYPE: The Puerto Rican Shangela
FAN-FAVOURITE PERFORMANCE: "I'm Outta Love" by Anastacia

Darienne Lake

"Two tons of fun of twisted steel and sex appeal."

WHAT'S THE T?

Emerging in August of 1990, Rochester's Miss Darienne Lake (Greg Meyer) has entertained audiences on stage and screen since, with club shows as well as appearances on iconic 90's chat shows. Her appearance on *Ricki Lake* with drag daughter and *Drag Race* alum Pandora Boxx in an episode named "Get a grip doll... you're too fat to be a drag queen" demonstrates the brilliantly crazy world of both 90's drag and 90's trash TV! After years of auditioning for *Drag Race*, Darienne Lake finally made the cut in the sixth season where she proved that a big girl can not only hold her own among the slighter queens from both a style and comedy angle. Following her top 4 performance on the *Race*, Darienne has toured as part of the Battle Of The Seasons Tour and even appeared on the *Christmas Queens* album in 2015 in a group performance with Pandora Boxx and fellow New Yorker Ivy Winters.

QUICK STATS

DRAG RACE: Season 6
RANKING: 4th place
SIGNATURE LOOK: Plus-size Pinup Realness
TYPE: Campy Glamour Queen
FAN-FAVOURITE PERFORMANCE: "Hello" by Martin Solveig ft. Dragonette

Dax Exclamationpoint

"What's up nerds?"

WHAT'S THE T?

A queen with roots in Savannah, Georgia, Dax Exclamationpoint (Dax Martin) began creating her drag persona in response to what she felt was a tired drag scene, harnessing her comic book fandom and club-kid creativity to break the mould. Drag mother to Season 7's winner Violet Chachki, Dax was cast in the eighth season of the *Race* where she excelled in a Hello Kitty costume challenge but gave an unfortunately weak lip-sync performance to the iconic "I Will Survive" by Gloria Gaynor against Laila McQueen. Both queens were told to sashay away in the second-ever double elimination on *Drag Race*. Dax continues to bring her brand of exquisitely created superhero and villainess looks to stages across the United States, joining Phi Phi O'Hara as one of *Drag Race*'s premier cosplay queens.

QUICK STATS

DRAG RACE: Season 8
RANKING: 11th/12th place
SIGNATURE LOOK: Superhero Showgirl Realness
TYPE: Cosplay Queen of All Nerds
FAN-FAVOURITE PERFORMANCE: "Baby's On Fire" by Die Antwoord

We're all born naked and the rest is DRAG

Delta Work

"I'm not worried about you,
I'm not worried about you and
I'm NOT worried about you!"

WHAT'S THE T?

A well-loved queen of the Southern California drag scene for over two decades, Delta Work (Gabriel Villarreal) was named by a fellow queen after a stint as Suzanne Sugarbaker (played by Delta Burke) in a *Designing Women* drag show. After many years as a longtime cast member of the *Dreamgirls Revue*, Delta was cast in the third season of *Drag Race* where she proved that a big girl can serve beautiful and polished runway looks, the house down! A "Heather" with a cutting sense of wit, Delta worked alongside new friends like Manila Luzon and her longtime sister Raja – the queen who first put her on stage – to give a strong performance in the competition, until falling flat in the comedy challenge. Delta Work continues to entertain across California and the United States and is currently serving as a creative producer and Ru's principal wig stylist on *RuPaul's Drag Race*.

QUICK STATS

DRAG RACE: Season 3
RANKING: 7th place
SIGNATURE LOOK: Living Pinup Realness
TYPE: The Seasoned Queen
FAN-FAVOURITE PERFORMANCE: "God Warrior Medley" by Various

Derrick Barry

"It's Derrick, bitch!"

WHAT'S THE T?

Put simply: Derrick Barry is the undisputed world's best Britney Spears drag impersonator. Initially impersonating Britney on a Halloween outing in 2003, Derrick has made an entire career out of emulating the princess of pop on The Strip in shows like *Frank Marino's Divas Las Vegas* ever since. After an unsuccessful audition for Season 7 of *Drag Race* and appearances on *America's Got Talent*, Derrick Barry was finally cast on the eighth season where she put his best foot forward as a drag performer, instead of just a Britney impersonator. While a well known star before even making it onto the *Race*, Derrick had to work hard to prove that her drag performance, costuming, acting and comedy skills were up to scratch with on-screen rival Bob The Drag Queen. After putting up a strong fight in the *Race* and bearing her soul as a seasoned performer changing up their drag, Derrick placed fifth in the competition. Following her season, Derrick has continued to build the drag identity of "Derrick Barry" and has forged a new career as a drag princess of pop with her hot club single "Boom Boom".

QUICK STATS

DRAG RACE: Season 8
RANKING: 5th place
SIGNATURE LOOK: Britney Spears Realness
TYPE: The Vegas Vixen
FAN-FAVOURITE PERFORMANCE: "Work Bitch" by Britney Spears

QUICK STATS

Season 5 | *All Stars* 2

4th place | Co-runner Up

Released directorial and solo single debut "Supersonic"; featured model on *Skin Wars*; guest host on Logo's *Gay For Play* game show featuring RuPaul; sickening runway model for LA-based designer Marco Marco; stars in WOW Presents web series *Detox's Life Rehab*

Thierry Mugler meets *Jem and the Holograms* Realness

The Style Icon

"I Look to You"
by Whitney Houston

"I am the queen bee so eat it up and crown it!"

Detox

WHAT'S THE T?

A long-time star of the WeHo drag scene, Detox – the alter ego of Matthew Sanderson – channels retro 80s style while opting for a performance style where this aesthetic is matched with a perfectly kitsch show sensibility. In her showtime staple "Nothing's Gonna Stop Us Now" by Starship, Detox marries Kim Cattrall's *Mannequin* with an outlandish 80s power suit and a frizzed weave for a perfectly camp power ballad performance. Prior to her appearance on *RuPaul's Drag Race*, Detox was a member of Californian band Tranzkuntinental alongside fellow *Drag Race* alumni Willam and Kelly Mantle.

In the lead up to her season of *Drag Race*, Detox was easily the most recognised personality to enter that race after a popular run of hit singles and music videos with her band DWV. Their 2013 single "Boy Is a Bottom" with over 20 million views, set the bar high for Detox, who only won one main challenge in her run on the show. Showing her ass literally and figuratively on the main stage, Detox channelled her camp lip-sync style in all of her Lip-sync for Your Life performances including the iconic face off with Jinkx Monsoon to Yma Sumac's "Malambo No. 1". Her unexpected monochrome appearance at the Season 5 finale cemented Detox's status as one of the most stylish and fierce queens ever to compete in the *Race*.

After touring internationally as a solo performer after the breakup of DWV and slaying the Marco Marco runway during Los Angeles Fashion Week year after year, Detox returned to compete in the second season of *All Stars* executing her unique sense of style and drag to place as a runner up with Katya.

"Category is: Cheesecake!"

WHAT'S THE T?

Having been doing drag for about four years before her appearance on the fourth season of *RuPaul's Drag Race*, DiDa Ritz (Xavier Hairston) worked the stages of Chicago, inspired by drag mother Lady Tajma Hall. Always buoyant and bubbly in the workroom and on stage, DiDa won over audiences in the *Race* with her now iconic lip-sync against The Princess of Natalie Cole's "This Will Be (An Everylasting Love)" in front of Natalie herself (she didn't want Natalie "leaving saying that drag queen did a horrible job on my song"). Coasting through the competition safely through to 6th place, DiDa continues to entertain American audiences alongside her *Drag Race* sisters.

QUICK STATS

DRAG RACE: Season 4
RANKING: 6th place
SIGNATURE LOOK: Wendy Williams Knowles Realness
TYPE: "The Legs of Halsted"
FAN-FAVOURITE PERFORMANCE: "Ego" by Beyoncé

Eureka O'Hara

"I'll eat you."

WHAT'S THE T?

A young yet seasoned Tennessee queen of the pageant scene, Eureka O'Hara (David Huggard) has built a drag career that pushes the boundaries of what a plus-sized queen is expected to do. A high-energy dancing diva and Miss East Coast USofA at Large 2013, Eureka appeared on our screens in the ninth season of the *Race* pitted against fellow pageant competitor Trinity Taylor, priming audiences for what could be a pageant rivalry to match that of Alyssa Edwards and Coco Montrese. Though performing strongly in the Lady Gaga and "Draggily Ever After" challenges, it was a knee injury caused by the cheerleading challenge that slowed down Eureka's streak and prompted RuPaul to ask her to leave the competition to rest, refocus and return in the tenth cycle of the competition. Knowing the level of polish and performance ability Eureka has, audiences are keen to see this queen return!

QUICK STATS

DRAG RACE: Season 9
RANKING: 11th place
SIGNATURE LOOK: Pageant Perfection Realness
TYPE: The High-energy Plus-size Diva
FAN-FAVOURITE PERFORMANCE: "It's My Time/Booty"
by Martha Wash/Jennifer Lopez

Farrah Moan

"Farrah Moan: One look and your mind is blown!"

WHAT'S THE T?

A young showgirl with an expensive taste for feathers and rhinestones, Farrah Moan's drag is not only inspired by the glitz and glamour of old Hollywood, but fetish fashion. A fan-favourite from the outset, Farrah (Cameron Clayton) competed in Season 9 of *Drag Race* not only blinding audiences with her highlighter but her beauty, bringing to the runway shimmering and glowing looks including an impeccable replica of Madonna's Super Bowl XLVI costume. While Farrah wasn't able to take home the crown, she showed that she was ready to grow and that there is a bright future ahead for the Texas-born showgirl.

QUICK STATS

DRAG RACE: Season 9
RANKING: 8th place
SIGNATURE LOOK: Highlighted-for-the-back-row Realness
TYPE: The Retro Glam Showgirl
FAN-FAVOURITE PERFORMANCE: "I Want To Be Loved By You"
by Sinead O'Connor

Gia Gunn

"Absolutely!"

WHAT'S THE T?

Landing fresh off the boat direct from a little trip in Asia like fresh tilapia, Chicago's Gia Gunn (Gia Ichikawa) has been entertaining audiences in drag since she was seven years old, which is when she started performing in traditional Japanese kabuki theatre as an *onnagata* (male actors who played women's roles). While "feeling her oats" in the sixth season of *Drag Race* Gia lit up screens with her countless catchphrases and turned out fabulous looks on the main stage before fatefully meeting her match in a lip-sync battle against her new sister Laganja Estranja. Following her appearance on the *Race*, Gia has gone from strength to strength professionally – touring the world, releasing a single with Alaska ("Stun" in 2017) – as well as personally, by overcoming her struggles with gender identity and transitioning into the absolutely stunning woman she is today.

QUICK STATS

DRAG RACE: Season 6
RANKING: 10th place
SIGNATURE LOOK: Banjee Glam Geisha Realness
TYPE: The Fresh Tilapia Queen
FAN-FAVOURITE PERFORMANCE: "Kabuki Ru Girl Mix" by Various

Ginger Minj

WHAT'S THE T?

Hailing from Leesburg, Florida, Joshua Eads-Brown has performed in the pageant circuit as Ginger Minj across the South for the best part of the 2010s earning her the titles of Miss Gay United States 2013 and Miss National Comedy Queen 2012. Inspired by Ginger, her favourite character on the 60s TV show *Gilligan's Island*, Minj had performed in the theatre since the age of four. A young queen in love with the classic funny ladies of yesteryear, she hosted *Broadway Brunch* in 2013 at Hamburger Mary's in Orlando – a full-scale musical production with a cast of fifteen with drag sister The Minx.

Following performances in the Orlando theatre scene in shows including *Chicago*, *Gypsy* and *The Wiz*, Ginger Minj competed in the seventh season of *Drag Race*. A plus-size queen and fan-favourite Ginger harnessed all her theatrical gusto to win the musical theatre challenge and give a memorable tribute to John Waters' *Pink Flamingos* in the parody "Eggs". Her strong performance in the competition pushed her to the final three where she came in as co-runner up with Pearl leading to her casting on the second season of *All Stars*. Although she didn't last long in the *All Star* race, she gave a fabulous vocal performance in the talent show extravaganza.

Following in the footsteps of *Drag Race* alumni Jinkx Monsoon, Ginger Minj has taken her powerful vocal ability, showgirl prowess and love for the classic era of cinema and created *Crossdresser for Christ* – a confessional musical chronicling her own drag evolution and life story.

> "I'm a crossdresser for Christ. I'll have you down on your knees..."

QUICK STATS

DRAG RACE:
Season 7 | *All Stars 2*

RANKING:
Co-runner Up | 8th place

POST DRAG RACE:
Toured her musical comedy
Crossdresser for Christ in 2015;
released debut album *Sweet T*
in 2016

SIGNATURE LOOK:
Glamour Toad Realness

TYPE:
The Comedy Queen of
the South

**FAN-FAVOURITE
PERFORMANCE:**
"The Edge of Glory"
by Lady Gaga

Honey Mahogany

"People get down on San Francisco... but there is so much beauty there – have you seen Honey Mahogany?"

WHAT'S THE T?

A creative yet socially conscious queen and the first ever from San Francisco to be cast on *Drag Race*, Honey Mahogany (Alpha Mulugeta) began her drag career while studying, co-founding Berkeley University's *Next Top Drag Performer* on-campus contest. Influenced by 60's and 70's glamour, Honey's appearance on the fifth season of the *Race* was short-lived – cancelled by the collection of kaftans that she wore on the main stage runway. While not getting a chance to showcase her vocal talents on the show, Honey Mahogany has continued to gag her fans with dance singles "It's Honey" and went on to released her own EP in 2014 titled *Honey Love*.

QUICK STATS

DRAG RACE: Season 5
RANKING: 10th/11th place
SIGNATURE LOOK: Bed Bath & Beyond Realness
TYPE: San Fran Glamour Queen
FAN-FAVOURITE PERFORMANCE: "It's Honey" by Honey Mahogany

India Ferrah

"Get her off of me!"

WHAT'S THE T?

An All American Goddess pageant winner before her 21st birthday in 2008, Virginia's India Ferrah (Shane Richardson) had learned the ropes of entertaining and snatching pageant crowns long before other queens could legally drink! After unsuccessfully auditioning for the first two seasons of *Drag Race* India (and her iconic $600 breastplate) was cast in the third season where she brought a sense of old-school glamour and new-school dance and performance style to the runway. A fumble in the "QNN" news reporter challenge saw India eliminated early in the contest, but inspired by criticism of her time on the show, India Ferrah moved in Las Vegas in 2012 where she has elevated her drag to a true showgirl status and is now considered one of the top performers on The Strip.

QUICK STATS

DRAG RACE: Season 3
RANKING: 10th place
SIGNATURE LOOK: Breast Plate Babe Realness
TYPE: High-glam Dancing Queen
FAN-FAVOURITE PERFORMANCE: "Tens Medley" by Jennifer Lopez & Various

Ivy Winters

"Ivyyyyyyyyyyyyy Winterrrrrrrrrrrrrs!"

WHAT'S THE T?

An actor, singer, former clown and having worked as a costumier in New York City dressing queens including Lady Bunny and Manila Luzon, Ivy Winters (Dustin Winters) is easily one of the strongest contestants to have ever competed in the *Race*. Demonstrating her style and circus artistry, Ivy stomped the runway in intricate costumes ranging from *Victor/Victoria* recreations to a newspaper cocktail dress to a larger-than-life butterfly on stilts! One of the nicest queens on *Drag Race*, Ivy snatched the title of Miss Congeniality, toured the word with the Battle of The Seasons Tour in 2016 and even clay-animated the music video for her Christmas single "Elfy Winters Night".

QUICK STATS

DRAG RACE: Season 5
RANKING: 7th place (Miss Congeniality)
SIGNATURE LOOK: High Concept Couture Realness
TYPE: The Creative Circus Queen
FAN-FAVOURITE PERFORMANCE: "Titanium" by Sia

Drag term

FOR THE GODS

A way to describe something as being done to perfection or to describe something as fabulous. For example: "Mariah's face is beat for the gods!"

Jade Jolie

"Serving up fish – tuna on a platter."

WHAT'S THE T?

Just like her namesake Angelina, Jade Jolie (Josh Green) serves fabulous mug, a polished aesthetic and larger-than-life looks for the children! Appropriately cast in what Alaska admits was the "Season of the Fish" (Season 5), Jade Jolie demonstrated not only sweet and colourful runway presentations but helped coin one of the most iconic catchphrases after a heated fight over human-hair wigs with Alyssa Edwards: "Girl – you had rolls all over the place in the back...". Feel free to clap back to that read! A self-proclaimed "gaymer" and fan of cosplay, Jade continues to harness pop culture to create shows and looks that are not only loved by club goers across the United States but to her 100,000 followers on Instagram each week.

QUICK STATS

DRAG RACE: Season 5
RANKING: 8th place
SIGNATURE LOOK: Lisa Frank Realness
TYPE: The Kaleidoscopic Queen
FAN-FAVOURITE PERFORMANCE: "Harley Quinn Medley" by Various

Jade Sotomayor

"Jade is definitely my alter-ego ... she has more balls than I do!"

WHAT'S THE T?

Having worked for years as a professional dancer and choreographer in Chicago, David Sotomayor made his debut as Jade in 2003, inspired by the Latin queens of pop, particularly Jennifer Lopez. Utilising her skills as a dancer and her fabulous Latin flair, Jade gave a solid performance in the very first season of *Drag Race*, showcasing her dance abilities in the girl group challenge and her soft side in the "MAC Viva-Glam" challenge. Jade has built on her status as one of the original Racers with shows across the States, on the Al and Chuck cruises and with continuing the growth of her choreography portfolio.

QUICK STATS

DRAG RACE: Season 1
RANKING: 6th place
SIGNATURE LOOK: J-To-Tha-L-O Realness
TYPE: Latina Queen of Dance
FAN-FAVOURITE PERFORMANCE: "I Need Your Love"
by Calvin Harris ft. Ellie Goulding

My goal is to always come from a place of

LOVE...

but sometimes you just have to break it down for a

motherf**ker

Jaidynn Diore Fierce

"No ma'am, no ham, no pam,
no cauliflower, no corn bread,
no green beans!"

WHAT'S THE T?

Starting her drag career at the age of 22, Jaidynn Diore Fierce (Christopher Williams) rocked the Nashville drag scene before bringing her larger-than-life vibrancy and edgy performance style to the main stage of *RuPaul's Drag Race* in Season 7. A pageant queen with one hell of a mug, Jaidynn brought the energy each week in the competition and while having to lip-sync for her life three times she showed audiences exactly why a big girl can hold it with the rest of them! Following her time on the *Race* Jaidynn has focussed on her collaborations with WOW Presents and her own channel on YouTube, creating *Drag Race* after-show reviews and makeup tutorials.

QUICK STATS

DRAG RACE: Season 7
RANKING: 8th place
SIGNATURE LOOK: Outerspace City Babe Realness
TYPE: Curvy Queen of Dance
FAN-FAVOURITE PERFORMANCE: "Single Ladies" by Beyoncé

Jasmine Masters

"No tea, no shade, no pink lemonade!"

WHAT'S THE T?

An old-school queen with so much new-school relevance and a meme-able sense of humour like no other, California's Jasmine Masters (Martell Robinson) has spent over 20 years honing her skills as a masterful queen of comedy and impersonation; her Patti LaBelle is EVERYTHING! Having already won over YouTube audiences with her "I'm Jasmine Masters and I have something to say..." series, RuPaul decided, as she was one of her own favourite performers, that it was time for Jasmine to compete in the *Race*. Though she floundered in the competition, her catchphrases and impeccable sense of humour won over audiences even if she was dubbed "the poster child of discontent". Following her time on the *Race*, Jasmine has continued to work and "get her jush" (check out her Instagram for explanations on this one!) in the Southern California drag circuit and has found new fans in her viral videos after Justin Bieber and other celebrities re-circulated snippets of her iconic rants.

QUICK STATS

DRAG RACE: Season 7
RANKING: 12th place
SIGNATURE LOOK: Patti Labelle Pageant Realness
TYPE: The Old School Diva
FAN-FAVOURITE PERFORMANCE: "Nene Leakes Mix" by Various

Drag term

GAG

To react intensely, as a result of shock.
To "gag" on a drag queen's "eleganza" is to
be absolutely floored by the fabulous artistry
and aesthetic that said queen is presenting.
The term can also be used as an exclamation
of satisfaction: "Gag!" – Manila Luzon.

Jaymes Mansfield

"These are my summer diamonds – some are diamonds, some are not!"

WHAT'S THE T?

Inspired by characters like Elvira and Pee Wee Herman, Milwaukee's Jaymes Mansfield (James Wirth) fleshed out her larger-than-life drag persona while building her YouTube channel over the last two years before being cast as one of the bubbly and camp queens of Season 9 of *Drag Race*. Unfortunately Jaymes didn't get much of a chance to show off her comedic talents nor her wacky wardrobe that has won over her social media fans, as she was eliminated first from the contest. Refusing to let the elimination put a hole in her sail, Jaymes has continued to produce content for her channel, building on an already impressive pre-*Race* fanbase with her costume and makeup tutorial videos and her incredibly well researched and presented *Drag HerStory* series.

QUICK STATS

DRAG RACE: Season 9
RANKING: 14th place
SIGNATURE LOOK: Teddy Bear Couture Realness
TYPE: The Hilarious Herstorian
FAN-FAVOURITE PERFORMANCE: "The Homecoming Queen's Got A Gun"
by Julie Brown

Jessica Wild

"I love that drink!"

WHAT'S THE T?

Born and raised in San Juan, Puerto Rico, Jessica Wild (Jose David Sierra) harnessed her skills as a dance choreographer and makeup artist to create a high-energy drag persona that saw her move to Miami to pursue a career as a showgirl. Chosen by the viewers online in a casting competition, Jessica appeared in the second of *RuPaul's Drag Race* serving not only wondrously wild costumes and hair, but a strong sense of confidence and humility. Performing strongly throughout her season, winning the "Rocker Chicks" live singing challenge, Jessica was closely beaten by the sensual performance of Tatianna in a Lip-sync For Your Life battle. Following her appearance on the *Race* Jessica Wild has continued to perform across the United States, released dance singles "You Like It Wild" and "Absolutely" and even impersonated pop star Selena on Bravo's *Watch What Happens Live*.

QUICK STATS

DRAG RACE: Season 2
RANKING: 6th place
SIGNATURE LOOK: Puerto Rican Pop Star Realness
TYPE: The Escandalo Sweetheart
FAN-FAVOURITE PERFORMANCE: "Absolutely" by Jessica Wild

Jiggly Caliente

"I went from a baked potato to a sweet potato!"

WHAT'S THE T?

With a name inspired by a Pokémon, New York's Jiggly Caliente (Bianca Castro) is a queen who serves ghetto fabulous like no other and can boast the title of winning her first drag contest on her first night of drag as Jiggly! As sweet as candy and as loud as a firecracker, Jiggly's appearance on the fourth season of *Drag Race* was met with both laughter at her jokes (and her baked potato couture runway in the first episode) and admiration for her fierceness in a lip-sync battle. While her runways didn't always win over the judges, Jiggly kept audiences gagging for her onscreen puffs with her fellow queens, never letting the fans down on seeing the fiery Filipina hold it down with the shadiest of queens in the *Untucked* lounge. Since competing on the *Race*, Jiggly has toured the world, released a rap track on the *Christmas Queens* album and came out as transgender, inspiring her fans far and wide to live their truth.

QUICK STATS

DRAG RACE: Season 4
RANKING: 8th place
SIGNATURE LOOK: Straight off the Subway Realness
TYPE: The NYC Asian Plus Size Barbie
FAN-FAVOURITE PERFORMANCE: "R.E.S.P.E.C.T" by Naturi Naughton

QUICK STATS

DRAG RACE:
Season 5

RANKING:
Winner

POST DRAG RACE:
Toured her off-Broadway musical comedy *The Vaudevillians* internationally; released cabaret albums *The Inevitable Album* (2014) and *ReAnimated* (2015); starred as the subject of documentary film and web series *Drag Becomes Him* (2015)

SIGNATURE LOOK:
Jewish MILF Realness

TYPE:
The Broadway Queen

FAN-FAVOURITE PERFORMANCE:
"Malambo No.1" by Yma Sumac

"I'm Seattle's youngest MILF."

Jinkx Monsoon

WHAT'S THE T?

Performing in drag for the first time at 15, Jerick Hoffer began his on-stage career with performances at underage nightclub Escape and dance club The Streets in his hometown of Portland, Oregon. Following a move to Seattle, Jinkx Monsoon emerged in a series of Funny or Die webisodes called *Monsoon Season*. A queen of all media and stage platforms, Jinkx continued her work in musical theatre with appearances in *Spring Awakening* and *Rent* as well as taking the title role in *Hedwig and the Angry Inch* in 2013. Prior to her appearance on *Drag Race* Jinkx became the subject of YouTube docu-series *Drag Becomes Him* exploring her life as Jerick and as Jinkx. This web series led to a film adaptation in 2015.

Inspired by the high-concept characterisation of Season 4 winner Sharon Needles, Monsoon was inspired to audition and thus landed a position on the fifth season of *Drag Race*. A dark horse throughout, Jinkx was contantly pressured by fellow competitors and judges on the merits of her costuming and makeup skills. However, she perservered to prove that she didn't need to be the fishiest, most glamorous queen – she was a superstar in her own right. Not only winning the main challenges for the "Snatch Game" (in her iconic performance of Little Edie Beale) and "Drama Queens", Jinkx went on to take the crown over fan-favourite Alaska and pageant superstar Roxxxy Andrews.

Following her win, Jinkx worked on bringing her show *The Vaudevillians* to a wider audience. Through major performances of the show off-broadway and as part of Sydney Mardi Gras, Jinkx demonstrated that she is a different kind of winner to her predecessors – she's the drag Andrew Lloyd Webber!

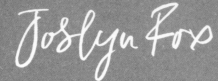

Joslyn Fox

"Keep it foxy – wonk wonk!"

WHAT'S THE T?

As a musical theatre kid only 20 years old, Patrick Joslyn discovered that his love of pop stars, hair and makeup artistry and music editing could be forged into an exciting career as Joslyn Fox – the stone cold fox of Massachusetts. Having auditioned four times for the show, Joslyn made her way onto Season 6 of *Drag Race* where she was immediately poised to compete with her personal drag idol Courtney Act. The self proclaimed "black horse", Joslyn worked her way through the competition with a sense of fun and positivity that may not have won her the title of Miss Congeniality, but won the hearts of viewers who were by her side as she gave her surprise wedding vows at the live Season 6 Reunion – with Mama Ru presiding over the ceremony of course! Joslyn Fox has continued to enjoy success as a touring Racer and starred in Bianca Del Rio's debut film *Hurricane Bianca*.

QUICK STATS

DRAG RACE: Season 6
RANKING: 6th place
SIGNATURE LOOK: Glamourpuss Realness
TYPE: The Stone Cold Fox
FAN-FAVOURITE PERFORMANCE: "Medley" by Janet Jackson

Drag term

GEISH

A term originated from Geisha – a Japanese female entertainer – "geish" refers to a drag queen's makeup and wardrobe. To be completely dressed in drag can be described as "in geish". In Season 6, Vivacious referred to Gia Gunn as "still a lady-boy, in or out of geish" referring to her feminine character while out of drag.

Jujubee

WHAT'S THE T?

Born from the drag scene of Boston, Massachusetts, Jujubee – the creation of Airline Inthyrath – was the creative fusion of her many years of studying theatre at the University of Massachusetts and her cultural upbringing as a Laotian American. Jujubee's aesthetic is often giving a cheeky nod to her Asian heritage while fusing traditional drag aesthetic and a slick street style.

A star from the second season of *Drag Race*, Jujubee won the hearts of the public despite never winning a main challenge. Her quick wit, warm disposition and cut-throat reading skills – "Miss Tyra, was your barbecue cancelled? Your grill is fucked up!" – pushed the Laotian goddess through to the top three of the competition. Described as the first lady of lip-sync, Jujubee is one of the most iconic performers in the history of *RuPaul's Drag Race* and despite having been in the bottom two five times, never lost a single lip-sync. Her performances to "Black Velvet" by Alannah Myles and Robyn's "Dancing on My Own" (with Raven on *All Stars*) remain undisputed demonstrations of incomparable drag performance.

Her additional appearances as a mainstay professor on the spin-offs *Drag U* and *Drag My Dinner* with Manila Luzon and Raven has helped boost Jujubee's social media reach, earning her a legion of fans on Facebook and Instagram giving her the status of one of the most followed queens from the earlier *Drag Race* seasons!

"I like long walks on the beach, big dicks and fried chicken."

Kandy Ho

"I hope you girls have got a sweet tooth 'cause Kandy's in the motherfucking house!"

WHAT'S THE T?

Hailing from YouTube-famous *The Doll House* – a Puerto Rican drag troupe of glamazons with out-of-this-world performance skills – is Kandy Ho (Frank Diaz), a pageant queen who made it onto the seventh season of *Drag Race*. Championed by her viral performances online, fans were eager to see Kandy take charge on the main stage of *Drag Race* only to be met with lacklustre performances in the acting-challenge heavy season. A gorgeous queen with a slick sense of choreography and show production, Kandy has continued to perform across the United States and Puerto Rico with her dance troupe.

QUICK STATS

DRAG RACE: Season 7
RANKING: 10th place
SIGNATURE LOOK: Glamour Ho Realness
TYPE: The All-powerful Performer
FAN-FAVOURITE PERFORMANCE: "Robotika" by Various

Mrs Kasha Davis

"There's always time for a cocktail!"

WHAT'S THE T?

Inspired by the character of Miss Richfield 1981 and under the guidance of drag mother Naomi Kane, Mrs Kasha Davis (Ed Popil) has become one of Rochester, New York's shining drag starlets alongside sisters Pandora Boxx and Darienne Lake. A laugh-out-loud kinda gal with a slick singing ability and a penchant for boxed wine, Kasha auditioned for all six previous seasons of *Drag Race* before finally being cast in the seventh, where she won audiences with her effervescent character and high-glamour housewife aesthetic. One of the "bitter old lady brigade" Kasha nailed the "Glamazonian Airways" challenge bringing to audiences a strong sense of old-school camp and kitsch to a season full of new-school Instagram famous queens. While her exit was untimely and the result of a stumble hosting the "Despy Awards", her return in the "Conjoined Queens" challenge alongside Despy co-host Katya was a *Banger Sisters* dream come true – with the two's conjoined-crotch-couture reminding audiences the value of good ole-fashioned crass drag. Since her time on *Drag Race* Mrs Kasha Davis has continued to evoke belly laughs online with web series *Life with the Davises* (co-starring Mr Davis!) and her first one-woman world-touring cabaret show *There's Always Time For A Cocktail*.

QUICK STATS

DRAG RACE: Season 7
RANKING: 11th place
SIGNATURE LOOK: Real Housewife of Rochester Realness
TYPE: The Mother Hen
FAN-FAVOURITE PERFORMANCE: "Cocktail" by Mrs Kasha Davis

QUICK STATS

DRAG RACE:
Season 7 | *All Stars* 2

RANKING:
5th place (Miss Congeniality) |
Co-runner Up

POST DRAG RACE:
Performs "12 Days of Christmas"
on the *Christmas Queens* album
(2015); featured on RuPaul's
single "Read U Wrote U" (2016);
administers a weekly dose of
laughs alongside Trixie Mattel
on their hugely popular
webseries *UNHhhh*

SIGNATURE LOOK:
Russian Bombshell Realness

TYPE:
The Cold War Comedy
Sweetheart

FAN-FAVOURITE
PERFORMANCE:
"All That Jazz" (In Russian) from
Chicago (Original Soundtrack)

"I'm just
your average
run-of-the-mill
Russian bisexual
transvestite
hooker."

WHAT'S THE T?

Katya Zamolodchikova – everyone's favourite Russian doll – was born from the mind of Boston's Brian McCook. Inspired by the comedy genius of Amy Sedaris, Tracey Ullman and Maria Bamford, and Russian songstress Alla Pugacheva, Katya's humour is the perfect blend of random hilarity and Soviet sass. A high concept character like Tammie Brown or Sharon Needles, Katya sees herself as a "retired kindergarten teacher that becomes a street-walking psychic crime fighter who's also battling depression and schizophrenia".

One of the front runners from the get go, Katya served not only glamour but camp in her performances throughout *Drag Race*. An early Lip-sync for Your Life performance to Olivia Newton-John's "Twist of Fate" in a perfectly floral patterned air hostess outfit was enough fire under Katya to inspire very strong performances in the John Waters inspired "Divine Inspiration", "Ru Hollywood Stories" and "Prancing Queens" challenges. Although coming in fifth place, Katya took out the title of Miss Congeniality for Season 7.

As a fan-favourite of her season, Katya found new fame online with her outrageously bonkers web series *RuGRETS* and *RuFLECTIONS* but it truely boomed when she teamed up in 2016 with fellow racer Trixie Mattel in their World of Wonder produced series *UNHhhh* – a brilliantly random segment where the two talk about whatever they want, because it's their show and not yours!

Katya returned stronger than ever in the second *All Stars* season winning three main challenges, placing as a runner-up alongside Detox, reminding audiences that she's "the only high class Russian whore" to take the drag world (and your dad) by storm.

Drag term

HALLELOO

An interjection to express happiness or praise, much like the word "hallelujah", and much like "yass!" or "werk!" is used by drag queens and gay men alike today. If you've caught any of Season 3 you will have heard the word at least once by Shangela.

Kelly Mantle

"Don't they know who I think I am?"

WHAT'S THE T?

Anyone who's watched American television in the last fifteen years or so will have caught a glimpse of drag actress extraordinaire Kelly Mantle. Appearing on shows like *Nip/Tuck* (alongside *Drag Race* sister Willam), *LAPD Blue*, *The New Normal* and *Curb Your Enthusiasm*, Kelly Mantle has built a career as a go-to queen when casting drag performers on screen, but she has also built a solid career as a live performer with band Tranzkuntinental. Possibly one of the strongest 'first-out' of the *Race*, Season Six was unfortunately a short ride for Mantle, who's bacon-esque blouse didn't win over the judges in the first week costuming challenge. Following the *Race*, Kelly has continued to pursue her music career with single "Keyboard Courage" as well as her acting career with a performance in 2014's *Confessions of a Womanizer*, which made headlines as the film's producers sought to nominate Mantle for both supporting actor and actress considerations at the Academy Awards for her performance being a gender-fluid person.

QUICK STATS

DRAG RACE: Season 6
RANKING: 13th place
SIGNATURE LOOK: Drag Rocker Realness
TYPE: The Television Queen
FAN-FAVOURITE PERFORMANCE: "My Neck My Back (Lick It)"
by Kelly Mantle

Kennedy Davenport

"I didn't die, bitch, I crystallized
and now I'm a glamazon bitch,
ready for the runway."

WHAT'S THE T?

Hailing from the legendary Davenport dynasty of Texas, Kennedy Davenport
(Reuben Asberry Jr.) has built her drag career since the age of 16, working her
way through the pageant scene of the South under the guidance of her drag
mother Kelexis to win a swag of titles including Mid-America All American
Goddess 2013. A strong contender for the crown in the seventh season of
Drag Race, Kennedy won over audiences with a killer impersonation of Little
Richard in the "Snatch Game" and her high-kicking power-split lip-sync to Katy
Perry's "Roar" against Katya. Following her dream of incorporating live vocals
into her act, Kennedy Davenport has opened her first-ever live cabaret show
The Gospel According to Kennedy Davenport to fabulous reviews in 2017.

QUICK STATS

DRAG RACE: Season 7
RANKING: 4th place
SIGNATURE LOOK: Polished Pageant Queen Realness
TYPE: The Dancing Diva of Dallas
FAN-FAVOURITE PERFORMANCE: "Last Dance" by Donna Summer

Kenya Michaels

"I'm a little person, but I'm FIERCE... BITCH!"

WHAT'S THE T?

A gorgeous and effervescent Puerto Rican queen, Kenya Michaels (Kenya Olivera) gave her first ever female impersonation act as Celia Cruz at the age of 15 as a gift to her sister for her birthday. A creative queen with a killer dance ability and a strong sense of fierce, Kenya wowed both her fellow cast and audiences in the fourth season of *RuPaul's Drag Race* with her unmatched beauty in such a little package. Although safe throughout most of the competition, Kenya was eliminated after a wacky and frankly out-of-character impersonation of Beyoncé in the "Snatch Game" only to be brought back for the makeover challenge, which she lost in a now iconic lip-sync to "(You Make Me Feel Like) A Natural Woman" against Latrice Royale. Coming out as transgender following her time on the *Race*, Kenya has continued to produce and perform shows in Florida as well as release her own men's fashion line.

QUICK STATS

DRAG RACE: Season 4
RANKING: 5th place
SIGNATURE LOOK: Petite Beauty Queen Realness
TYPE: The Pint Sized Perra
FAN-FAVOURITE PERFORMANCE: "Shakira Medley" by Shakira

ALL SINS ARE FORGIVEN ONCE YOU START MAKING A LOT OF MONEY

Kim Chi

"Donut come for me!"

WHAT'S THE T?

Chicago's priestess of pastel with a taste for over-the-top high-concept fashion, Kim Chi (Sang-Young Shin) started playing with drag in 2012 with *Drag Race* sister Pearl, quickly perfecting her unique brand of often Asian-inspired drag. Exhibiting the sheer creativity, mastery and level of research skill that many Asian drag queens possess, Kim Chi appeared on the eighth season of *Drag Race* where she placed as runner-up, claiming two costume creation challenge wins and essentially slaying the main stage runway from week to week. Winning over audiences in the *Race* has only been the start for Kim Chi, who has gone on to release her own line of makeup with Sugar Pill, tour South Korea and star in her own web series *M.U.G.* with Naomi Smalls, reviewing makeup trends seen on fellow Drag Racers.

QUICK STATS

DRAG RACE: Season 8
RANKING: Co-runner Up
SIGNATURE LOOK: Pastel Fantasy Realness
TYPE: The Kawaii Queen
FAN-FAVOURITE PERFORMANCE: "Fat, Fem & Asian" by Lucian Piane

Kimora Blac

"Kimora Blac is everyone's sexual preference!"

WHAT'S THE T?

A huge fan of transformation, playing with drag from the age of 15, Las Vegas vixen Kimora Blac (Von Nguyen) has built a drag persona for more than ten years that sells seduction and sex like no other. An Instagram star boasting more than 200,000 fans, Kimora has channelled her inner Kim K not only in her aesthetic but in creating a brand of drag that leaves her fans wanting to gag on more of her incredible transformations from man to woman. While her time on the ninth season of *Drag Race* was short-lived, she managed to leave the competition with a connection to the drag community that she didn't feel she had prior as a working showgirl on the Vegas Strip. Kimora Blac continues to wow audiences with her porn star-meets-Kardashian realness and build a legacy with her Las Vegas sisters Coco Montrese, Farrah Moan and Derrick Barry.

QUICK STATS

DRAG RACE: Season 9
RANKING: 13th place
SIGNATURE LOOK: Body-ody-ody-suit Realness
TYPE: The Boujee Barbie
FAN-FAVOURITE PERFORMANCE: "Sex Shooter" by Cahill

Laganja Estranja

WHAT'S THE T?

A member of the legendary Haus of Edwards, Laganja Estranja (Jay Jackson) emerged from years working as a choreographer with Alyssa Edwards' Beyond Belief Dance Company in Dallas. Following a move to study in California, Laganja honed her drag talents alongside newcomer Adore Delano and went on to win a drag contest at Micky's in West Hollywood and subsequently a monthly guest spot alongside *Drag Race* alumni at the famed *Showgirls* drag night. A sickening dancer and performer, Laganja quickly took the LA drag scene by storm with her dancing troupe Barbie's Addiction.

Although still a newcomer to drag, Laganja was cast in the sixth season of *RuPaul's Drag Race* following in the footsteps of drag mother Alyssa Edwards and sister Shangela. While a fan-favourite from the outset, Laganja's performance through the season was green (pun intended) and lacked the experience of her competitors. Despite receiving a lot of tough love from the judges and Bianca Del Rio, Laganja went on to win one major challenge and finished eighth after two strong lip-syncs against Gia Gunn and Joslyn Fox.

Determined to prove her star quality and exceptional dance skills, Laganja has gone on to choreograph and perform alongside Miley Cyrus in the iconic 2015 MTV VMA performance, which starred over 30 drag performers. A star of World of Wonder's WOW Presents YouTube channel in shows *Alyssa's Secret* and *Bestie$ for Ca$h*, Laganja has also released her own solo single "Legs" and even developed her own marijuana-themed jewellery line.

"I'm too busy looking at my gorgeous body."

QUICK STATS

DRAG RACE:
Season 6

RANKING:
8th place

POST DRAG RACE:
Tours internationally with the Haus of Edwards alongside drag family Alyssa Edwards and Shangela; released single "Legs" (2015) with rapper Rye Rye; choreographed the Miley Cyrus performance of "Dooo It!" 2015 MTV Video Music Awards

SIGNATURE LOOK:
Mary Jane Girl Realness

TYPE:
The Sickening Stoner

FAN-FAVOURITE PERFORMANCE:
"Beyoncé Medley" (with Barbie's Addiction) by Beyoncé

Laila McQueen

"I'm the crossbreed between a cute stripper and a punk rock girl."

WHAT'S THE T?

Performing her first official drag gig the day after she turned 18, Gloucester's (Massachusetts) Laila McQueen (Tyler Devlin) spent her high school years building her drag skill set in art projects and rebelliously cross-dressing at parties. A self-proclaimed "bra and panties with a blazer" queen with a rabid lesbian fanbase, Laila appeared in the eighth season on *Drag Race* where she found herself in the bottom two in the first two episodes of the season, finally being eliminated in the shocking double elimination to "I Will Survive" with Dax Exclamationpoint. Following her time on the *Race*, Laila has worked with WOW Presents, creating makeup tutorial videos as well as viral content alongside previous *Drag Race* contestants.

QUICK STATS

DRAG RACE: Season 8
RANKING: 11th/12th place
SIGNATURE LOOK: Glam Goth Realness
TYPE: The #DeathSplat Queen
FAN-FAVOURITE PERFORMANCE: "Tainted Love" by Marilyn Manson

LaShauwn Beyond

"This is not RuPaul's Best Friend Race!"

WHAT'S THE T?

Coining one of the most famous lines of *Drag Race* doesn't happen every day but for LaShauwn Beyond (Jamall Jackson) it's only the tip of the impact this queen has made on the world of drag. Prior to her appearance on *Drag Race*'s fourth season, LaShauwn Beyond was well known as a costumier and seamstress from Florida who had previously worked for Season 4 sister Latrice Royale, creating sickening custom gowns. Despite turning out a sky-scraping "post apopkalakic" look in the first costume challenge, LaShauwn found herself eliminated after the wrestling challenge, which proved to be a feat too difficult for the seamstress extraordinaire. Following the *Race* LaShauwn Beyond spends more of her time behind the scenes turning out epic costumes and prom gowns; her Instagram account is to die for, and a must for any lover of a nude illusion gown!

QUICK STATS

DRAG RACE: Season 4
RANKING: 12th place
SIGNATURE LOOK: Out Of This World Hair Fantasy Realness
TYPE: The Seamstress Queen
FAN-FAVOURITE PERFORMANCE: "Radio" by Beyoncé

QUICK STATS

DRAG RACES:
Season 4 | *All Stars* 1

RANKINGS:
4th place (Miss Congeniality)
| 7th place

POST DRAG RACE:
Introduced and performed
"You Make Me Feel (Mighty
Real)" with Jennifer Hudson at
Fashion Rocks; released dance
singles "Weight" (2014) and
"Thick Thighs" (with Willam,
2015); officiates weddings and
civil ceremonies as a certified
marriage celebrant

SIGNATURE LOOK:
Diamante Diva Realness

TYPE:
The Large and in Charge Queen

FAN-FAVOURITE
PERFORMANCE:
"Weight" (Season 7 Grand Finale)
by Latrice Royale

"She is large
and in charge.
Chunky yet
funky."

Latrice Royale

WHAT'S THE T?

Raised in Compton, California, Timothy Wilcots' drag persona Latrice Royale emerged in the mid 1990s at the Fort Lauderdale club The Copa where she won her first amateur drag contest. A natural performer with incredible work ethic and captivating moves, Latrice competed in the pageant circuit winning the title of Miss Pride South Florida in 2004.

Latrice Royale won the hearts of fans across the globe after her performance on the fourth season of *Drag Race*. By not only being a "B.I.T.C.H." (Being in Total Control of Herself) but also as a formidable costumier, performer and all-round polished queen, Latrice powered her way to the top four of the competition and won the title of Miss Congeniality. Lip-sync performances against Kenya Michaels ("You Make Me Feel Like a Natural Woman") and DiDa Ritz ("I've Got to Use My Imagination") demonstrated a world-class style of classic drag artistry. In the months following, Latrice teamed up to form "Team Latrila" with Manila Luzon in the first season of *All Stars*, bringing back her timeless wit and warmth to the screen as a fan-favourite.

In the aftermath of her popularity on *Drag Race*, the now Florida-based Royale founded talent management firm All Starr Management, a 40-person strong team of talented drag acts, musicians and photographers including fellow Drag Racers Nina Flowers and Kennedy Davenport. Latrice has gone on to star in the Logo TV documentary *Gays in Prison* (2015) where she discussed her life behind bars prior to her appearance on *Drag Race*.

Lineysha Sparx

"So fierce, so flawless, so sparkling!"

WHAT'S THE T?

One of the most glamorous Puerto Rican queens to grace the main stage of *RuPaul's Drag Race*, Lineysha Sparx (Andy Trinidad), happens to also be one of the most appreciated queens out of drag as well... as far as trade is concerned! From the outset of Season 5, Lineysha demonstrated a masterful ability to create costumes out of almost anything, with her wallpaper couture receiving a rapturous response from the judges in the first episode. As the season went on, Lineysha's style and runway presentations wowed, but the language barrier that affected her Puerto Rican sisters on previous seasons caught up with her and sent her packing after a lacklustre Celia Cruz impersonation on the "Snatch Game". Still a young queen with a bright future, Lineysha continues to entertain audiences across the United States with her Latin glamour.

QUICK STATS

DRAG RACE: Season 5
RANKING: 9th place
SIGNATURE LOOK: Miss Puerto Rico Realness
TYPE: The Latina Glamazon
FAN-FAVOURITE PERFORMANCE: "Whine Up" by Kat DeLuna

Madame LaQueer

"Are we talking about beavers or... ewwwwwwwww!"

WHAT'S THE T?

Since commencing her drag career at the start of the new millennium, Madame LaQueer (Carlos Melendez) has built a drag empire of her own in Puerto Rico: producing shows; winning four pageants; and launching the careers of queens like fellow Racers April Carrión and Kandy Ho at her event *Queen of The Night*. Appearing in Season 4 of *Drag Race*, Madame won the "World's Trashiest Fighters" challenge at the start of the season with teammate Chad Michaels, but soon found herself in the bottom two after a poor performance in the acting challenge. Turning it out as a "pointer sister" performer ("'Pointer sisters' are the girls who just point during a lip-sync..." – Jiggly Caliente) to Pink's "Trouble", LaQueer was sent packing by Milan. Inspired to move to Southern California after her time on *Drag Race*, Madame LaQueer continues to entertain fans at famous drag spot Micky's in WeHo.

QUICK STATS

DRAG RACE: Season 5
RANKING: 9th place
SIGNATURE LOOK: 80's Villainess Realness
TYPE: The Fierce Face Queen
FAN-FAVOURITE PERFORMANCE: "Lean On Medley"
by Major Lazer & Various

Magnolia Crawford

"I'm just here for the exposure."

WHAT'S THE T?

A jet-setting queen by trade, Magnolia Crawford (Reynolds Engelhart) is a conceptual queen who is – intentionally – stylistically stuck in the late 1980's/early 1990's. The blonde-bombshell that prefers to be seen on computer screens rather than live on stage, was unfortunately eliminated on the first episode of Season 6 of *Drag Race*, after a less than inspired cow-pattered costume presentation on the main stage. After being met with negative criticism after the appearance on *Drag Race*, Engelhart decided to give the character of Magnolia Crawford a break and focus on his career as an air steward.

QUICK STATS

DRAG RACE: Season 6
RANKING: 14th place
SIGNATURE LOOK: Blonde-Bombshell Realness
TYPE: The Misunderstood Queen
FAN-FAVOURITE PERFORMANCE: "No One Tells A Queen What To Do"
by Magnolia Crawford & Adam Barta

Drag term

HEATHER

The opposite of a "booger", a "heather" is a way of describing a queen who is polished and fierce. In Season 3 "The Heathers" alliance consisted of Raja, Delta Work, Carmen Carrera and Manila Luzon – queens who self-identified as the strongest competitors in that *Race* due to their strengths in style, performance and all-round drag artistry.

Manila Luzon

WHAT'S THE T?

After his first stint in drag as Cruella de Vil at 19, Karl Westerberg created similarly wigged beauty Manila Luzon in the late 2000s as he appeared in the New York night life as a club queen with partner and *Drag Race* legend Sahara Davenport. Demonstrating a strong eye for fashion with her conceptual couture from the outset, Manila became a popular scene queen for her fun sense of costume construction and artistry.

Appearing in the third season of *Drag Race*, Luzon blitzed her way ahead of the competition in iconic couture ranging from Big Bird cosplay to pineapple ball gown realness to Louis Vuitton carrot-cake couture, some of which were created by later Drag Racer Ivy Winters. The winner of three main challenges and member of the feisty Heathers troupe consisting of Raja, Delta Work and Carmen Carrera, Luzon's strong work ethic and blend of glamour and camp pushed her to the top two of the contest, surrendering the crown to Raja. Her iconic performance of Donna Summer's "Macarthur Park" against Delta Work following the "Ru Ha Ha" challenge remains one of the strongest Lip-sync for Your Life performances in the herstory of the show.

In the years following, Manila became one of the first queens to release her own music as well as starring as a playable character in the iPhone App drag game *Dragopolis*. Luzon's eye for fashion has also enabled her to collaborate with fashion designers Viktor Luna (from *Project Runway*) as well as walk catwalks for LA designer Marco Marco on numerous occasions.

QUICK STATS

DRAG RACES:
Season 3 | *All Stars* 1

RANKINGS:
2nd place | 8th place

POST DRAG RACE:
Star of *RuPaul's Drag Race*
spin-offs *Drag U* and *Drag My Dinner*
with Raven and Jujubee; released
pop single "Hot Couture" (2012) and
dance track "Helen Keller"
(with Cazwell) (2014); featured
in television advertisement
"Red Ribbon Runway" raising
awareness for HIV/AIDs

SIGNATURE LOOK:
Black and Blonde
Beauty Realness

TYPE:
The Filipino Fashionista

FAN-FAVOURITE PERFORMANCE:
"MacArthur Park"
by Donna Summer

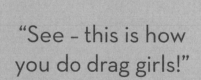

"See - this is how
you do drag girls!"

Drag term

THE HOUSE
DOWN

A phrase used at the end of sentences to describe "a lot" or a great amount; a very drawn out exclamation point. For example: "Trinity Taylor can dance the house down" (Trinity can dance!). "The house down" can be followed by other words like "boots" to draw out the strength of the exclamation.

Mariah Paris Balenciaga

"When it comes to going out in drag in the day time, I'm good... if it's right, it's right."

WHAT'S THE T?

Born from the hallowed ground that is the ballroom scene of Atlanta, Mariah Paris Balenciaga (Elijah Kelly) created her mystifying drag persona while working as a top celebrity hair stylist. Having "brought it to the ball" differently with each contest back home, Mariah was more than ready for the challenges of Season 3, even though she hadn't much experience performing in actual drag shows. Serving not only a fierce sense of style and "mug4dayz" (the name of Mariah's first dance single – as well as her Insta handle) on the show, but a slick sense of wit, Mariah worked her way to the middle of the pack after a stumble in the "Snatch Game" as a less than fierce Joan Crawford. Following the *Race*, Mariah has not only been teaching the children how to nail their first time at a ball as a professor on *RuPaul's Drag U*, but she's moved to LA and is now a star of the West Hollywood drag scene.

QUICK STATS

DRAG RACE: Season 3
RANKING: 9th place
SIGNATURE LOOK: Feathered Fish Realness
TYPE: The Ballroom Queen
FAN-FAVOURITE PERFORMANCE: "Your Body" by Christina Aguilera

Max

"I'm Max – a starlet on the rise!"

WHAT'S THE T?

Meeting at the cross-section of old Hollywood and Iggy Azalea, the silver-haired seductress of Season 7, Max Malanaphy took her first steps in drag in 2012 as Dr Frank-N-Furter in a Minneapolis production of *The Rocky Horror Show*. In the following years, Max dialled up the vamp to 11 as her drag persona morphed into the vintage vixen that appeared on *Drag Race* – wowing audiences with not only killer ensembles (her "Bleeding Heart" runway slays!) but an entrancing disposition that saw her soar through the competition. While failing to bring the laughs (and the "boos") with her impression of Sharon Needles in the "Snatch Game", Max found herself eliminated after a lip-sync against Jaidynn Diore Fierce. Looking at her time on the race as an audition for a future in drag, Max has continued to perform and serve up flawless looks for her Instagram fans.

QUICK STATS

DRAG RACE: Season 7
RANKING: 9th place
SIGNATURE LOOK: Sultry In Steel Realness
TYPE: The Silver Screen Beauty Queen
FAN-FAVOURITE PERFORMANCE: "I Put A Spell On You" from *Hocus Pocus*

Milan

"Colored Girl, why your base look like chalk?!"

WHAT'S THE T?

An accomplished actor, singer/songwriter and dancer in New York City prior to her appearance on Season 4, Milan (Dwayne Cooper) had not only starred in *Hairspray* on Broadway, but had gone viral with her 2006 parody video *Miss Cleo*, which garnered over 1.5 million views on YouTube. Through three Lip-sync for your Life contests, audiences were wowed by Milan's high-energy performance style as she "swiffered the floor with her taint", flipped wigs and vogued on her head like no contestant before. Performing as Milan has taken a backseat, but the consummate triple-threat Dwayne has continued his performance on stage and screen in *Unbreakable Kimmy Schmidt* and 2017's musical tour of *The Doo Wop Project*.

QUICK STATS

DRAG RACE: Season 4
RANKING: 9th place
SIGNATURE LOOK: Janelle Monae Realness
TYPE: The Broadway Queen
FAN-FAVOURITE PERFORMANCE: "The Miss Cleo Song" by Dwayne Milan

"Milk!
She does a body
good, girl."

QUICK STATS

DRAG RACE:
Season 6

RANKING:
9th place

POST DRAG RACE:
Star of her own World of
Wonder produced web series
Milk's LegenDAIRY Looks;
coverboy for *Hello Mr.* magazine
entitled "Dan Donigan: Meet
the Milk Man"; joined stars
like Bette Midler and Sandra
Bernhard as a model in the 2016
Marc Jacobs spring campaign

SIGNATURE LOOK:
Club Kid Chameleon Realness

TYPE:
The Creative Clown

**FAN-FAVOURITE
PERFORMANCE:**
"E.T. (Take Me Home)"
by Cash Cash

Milk

WHAT'S THE T?

In 2008 ex-competitive figure skater Daniel Donigan, inspired by his new boyfriend and friends' impromptu "10-minute-makeover" drag made his first ever drag transformation – a gender-fuck "Little Merman" fusion of male and female attire with a killer heel. Addicted to online makeup tutorials, Milk was soon born after a move to NYC where she was immediately snatched up by nightlife icon Susanne Bartsch – an old friend of RuPaul and the 90s club kids. Pumping out week after week of offbeat yet high-fashion looks, Milk and her drag posse the Dairy Queens took the New York drag scene by storm with their incomparable theme-oriented conceptual style of drag.

Milk's *Drag Race* audition tape was a rainbow wheel of innovative looks, comedic schtick and fresh creativity not seen before on the *Race* runway. Entering the workroom a statuesque flamenco-themed glamazon clown, Milk set the bar for her soon to be legendary looks which included her take on Pinocchio, Jon Benet Ramsey realness, RuPaul (the werkroom male Ru that is!) and the envelope-pushing bearded Gandalf moment in episode 1's runway. Expectedly punished by Michelle Visage's "When Will You Show Us Glamour" stick week in week out, Milk never succumbed to pressure to tame her creativity honouring her own sense of glamour and fabulousness until an untimely elimination in the sixth week of the competition.

Following *Drag Race*, Milk became a spokesmodel for the wacky and fun drag that had yet to be seen in six seasons of the *Race* and instantly won the following of both underground and bearded queens everywhere.

Mimi Imfurst

"Boo just 'cause you got a sugar daddy
who pays everything for you..."

WHAT'S THE T?

An insult comic extraordinaire with a long career as a DJ, hostess, theatre and drag performer, Mimi Imfurst (Braden Chapman) is "Jill of all trades" when it comes to the performing arts game. While a popular working New York queen before Season 3, Mimi famously found herself in hot water with fellow contestants and the rabid *Drag Race* fanbase as she (literally) picked up India Ferrah and threw the insults back at Shangela, in what are now iconic moments of the series. Such scenes lead to her casting in the first season of *All Stars* where the drama continued in the form of hostility from her teammate Pandora Boxx, leading to an early elimination. Following her two explosive *Drag Race* appearances, Mimi Imfurst has found great success on the pageant circuit, winning the title of Miss'd America (2016) and as a show producer creating the famous *Battle of The Seasons* and *Dragapalooza* live concert tours where she performed material from her solo record *The Fire* alongside Racers like the AAA Girls, Derrick Barry and Trixie Mattel.

QUICK STATS

DRAG RACE: Season 3 | *All Stars* 1
RANKING: 11th place | 12th place
SIGNATURE LOOK: Lady DJ Realness
TYPE: The Theatre Queen
FAN-FAVOURITE PERFORMANCE: "The Roast of Michelle Visage" by Mimi Imfurst

Miss Fame

"Greetings Earth Queens, I come in peace"

WHAT'S THE T?

Working as a well-respected makeup artist and editorial model for years before her appearance on the seventh season of *Drag Race*, Miss Fame (Kurtis Dam-Mikkelsen) entered the race as a fan-favourite with her out-of-this-world aesthetic. The self-proclaimed "Rolls Royce of Drag" brought to the show not only a slew of sickening makeup and costume creations, but revealed her country side – winning audiences over with her goofy and loveable personality before an elimination lip-sync against Pearl in the "Ugliest Drag" runway challenge. Immediately after her time on the show, Miss Fame took the challenge of taking her brand to new heights by not only releasing her debut solo record *Beauty Marked* (2015) and touring her makeup tutorials across the United States, but by forging an unprecedented relationship with L'Oréal as a spokesmodel where she walked the 2016 Cannes Film Festival Red Carpet as the first drag artist ever to grace that event.

QUICK STATS

DRAG RACE: Season 7
RANKING: 7th place
SIGNATURE LOOK: Rubber Doll Realness
TYPE: The Macquillage Mistress of Drag
FAN-FAVOURITE PERFORMANCE: "Primitive" by Richard Vission vs Luciana

Look at me —
a BIG OLD
BLACK MAN
under all of this makeup,
and if I can look
BEAUTIFUL
so can you

Monica Beverly Hillz

"Who you callin' ghetto?"

WHAT'S THE T?

Before appearing in the fifth season of *Drag Race*, Chicago's Monica Beverly Hillz had spent seven years building her drag persona, inspired by her love for dance and her passion for the fun and flirty side of the art form. Serving straight-up banjee girl realness in her runway performances and backstage in her *Untucked* spat with Serena ChaCha, it was the "Draggle Rock" challenge which challenged Monica's acting abilities and saw her sashay away. Just prior to her elimination, Monica bravely came out – not only to her fellow contestants and the judges, but the world – as transgender, educating audiences that "trans is who (she is) and drag is what (she does)". Following her time on the *Race*, Monica Beverly Hillz joined her *Drag Race* sisters onstage with Miley Cyrus at the VMA awards, continues to entertain in drag at clubs across the United States and now uses her experience with transitioning to inform and educate in online editorials and YouTube interviews.

QUICK STATS

DRAG RACE: Season 5
RANKING: 12th place
SIGNATURE LOOK: Fish From The Block Realness
TYPE: The Banjee Babe
FAN-FAVOURITE PERFORMANCE: "Hot Sugar" by Tamar Braxton

Morgan McMichaels

"You have no class and no manners... so go fix your hair, go fix your mug"

WHAT'S THE T?

West Hollywood icon Morgan McMichaels (Thomas White) started her drag career in 2002, curating a persona with an impeccable skillset of dance ability, makeup artistry and untouchable impersonation – inspired by and under the guidance of drag mother Chad Michaels. Entering the second season of *Drag Race* as a seasoned performer with best friend Raven, Morgan was one to beat as she won the first "Gone With The Window" costume challenge and gave a *shelarious* performance as an eccentric grandmother in the "Disco Extra Greasy Shortening" commercial challenge. After a stumble in the "Snatch Game" as an aesthetically correct – yet stiff-as-a-board – Pink and two power-packed lip-syncs, Morgan found herself eliminated a lot earlier than fans anticipated. In the years after *Drag Race*, Morgan McMichaels has spent her time solidifying her career as a full-time queen and building the Monday night at Mickey's in WeHo to be the epicentre of drag on the West Coast, while also acting as a professor in *Drag Race* spin off *Drag U* and appearing in her own WOW Presents webseries *Living For The Lip-sync*.

QUICK STATS

DRAG RACE: Season 2
RANKING: 8th place
SIGNATURE LOOK: #Booty4Dayz Realness
TYPE: The Inimitable Queen of Performance
FAN-FAVOURITE PERFORMANCE: "If I Were A Boy" by Beyoncé

Mystique Summers Madison

"Bitch I am from Chicago!"

WHAT'S THE T?

The original large and in charge *Drag Race* diva from the South, Mystique Summers Madison (Donté Sims) started performing in drag in 2005 and while competing in the Imperial Court pageant system, won the title of North Carolina All-American Goddess. With several pageants under her belt, Mystique was cast on Season 2 ready and thirsty to take the crown representing the big girls, serving Southern glamour and charm. While winning the "Chicken or What?" mini-challenge, Mystique found herself in the bottom two during the "Country Queens" challenge after a less than impressive "mall drag" interpretation of country realness – and sashayed away in a stage-splitting fierce exit. In the following years after her season of *Drag Race*, Mystique still performs in drag, touring the seas with the Al & Chuck Drag Stars cruises and has appeared in various WOW Presents viral videos.

QUICK STATS

DRAG RACE: Season 2
RANKING: 10th place
SIGNATURE LOOK: Two Piece and a Biscuit Realness
TYPE: The #Painted4Filth Diva
FAN-FAVOURITE PERFORMANCE: "Work It/Gossip Folks" by Missy Elliot

Drag term

JUDY

A Judy, or "good Judy", is a way to describe a gay male you would consider a very good or close friend. The term "Judy" originates from the gay slang "friend of Dorothy" – a euphemism for "gay", dating back as far as World War II. Dorothy in the *Wizard of Oz* was, of course, played by Judy Garland, thus signalling the evolution of the term over time.

Naomi Smalls

"Check your lipstick before you come for me!"

WHAT'S THE T?

Spending her junior years of high school watching *Drag Race*, Naomi Smalls (David Heppenstall) is truly a new-generation queen who has grown with the show as inspiration for her artistry and performance style. Winning *Raven's Raucous Roundup* drag contest in Pomona in 2013, Naomi made the decision to follow her mentor and participate in the eighth season of the *Race* as one of the youngest competitors that cycle. Bringing her brand of supermodel meets Studio 54 glamour to the runway, Naomi Smalls took out a top three position serving sickening runway presentations including her challenge winning – now iconic – "Wizards of Drag" scarecrow look. Naomi's performance of her final three track "Legs" wowed the audiences at the reunion and boasts over 1.5 million views on YouTube today! Still a young queen with a bright future, Naomi Smalls continues to tour across the world and stars alongside Race-mate Kim Chi in their makeup review web series *M.U.G.*

QUICK STATS

DRAG RACE: Season 8
RANKING: Co-runner Up
SIGNATURE LOOK: 90's Supermodel Realness
TYPE: The High-fashion Hood Rat
FAN-FAVOURITE PERFORMANCE: "Roses" by ABRA

Naysha Lopez

"Hola! The beauty is here!"

WHAT'S THE T?

A Chicago queen with an accomplished Latin dance career, Naysha Lopez (Fabian Rodriguez) spent the 13 years of her drag career before the *Race* slaying the stage and snatching crowns including the prestigious title of Miss Continental 2013. With a title that has been shared with the likes of icons Candis Cayne and Erica Andrews, Naysha entered Season 8 of *RuPaul's Drag Race* as a contestant to watch out for – but soon found herself eliminated in the first episode after a poor effort creating a look in the style of Season 1's "Drag On A Dime" thrift-shop-based design challenge. After a swift phone call from RuPaul following a double-elimination, this "rectangle girl of the world" returned to the competition for two more weeks before sashaying away for a second time following her less than groovy "Dragometry" live performance. Although not an America's Next Drag Superstar, Naysha Lopez has returned to taking home pageant trophies – including scoring the title of Miss New York Universo Latina USA 2017 – and continuing to tour "the beauty" across the United States.

QUICK STATS

DRAG RACE: Season 8
RANKING: 9th place
SIGNATURE LOOK: Pageant Princesa Realness
TYPE: #TheBeauty
FAN-FAVOURITE PERFORMANCE: "Ain't It Funny" by Jennifer Lopez

GIVE A DRAG QUEEN A FISH AND YOU FEED HER FOR A DAY; SHOW HER HOW TO BE *fishy* AND YOU FEED HER FOR A LIFETIME

Nicole Paige Brooks

"You know you want a taste of cherry pie!"

WHAT'S THE T?

The seductive Southern belle with charm that's sweeter than the taste of her cherry pie and as sharp as her acrylic toenails for days, Nicole Paige Brooks (Brian Christopher Pryor), from Atlanta, Georgia, began her successful career as a performer at 21 as part of a Halloween dare like many queens before her. Determined to improve her female impersonation act, Nicole was taken under the wing of drag mother Shawnna Brooks and her house, where she built the seasoned performer that appeared on the second season of *Drag Race*. A drag dad alongside Race-mate Tyra Sanchez, Nicole went into the *Race* with the goal of openly showing her son the career path that his dad had chosen, but was unfortunately eliminated in the second episode after a less than impressive "drunk Janice Dickinson-esque" strip show performance. The legend of Nicole Paige Brooks from Atlanta, Georgia, continues to echo in the hearts of Drag Racers and fans alike, as she continues to bring her self-proclaimed "X-Rated" brand of drag to nightclubs across the South and in videos on the WOW Presents network.

QUICK STATS

DRAG RACE: Season 2
RANKING: 11th place
SIGNATURE LOOK: Southern Fish Realness
TYPE: The Fan Favourite Diva of Atlanta, Georgia
FAN-FAVOURITE PERFORMANCE: "Shake It Off" by Taylor Swift

Nina Bo'Nina Brown

"Sue me!"

WHAT'S THE T?

Inspired by cartoons, video games and her love for larger-than-life booty pads, Nina Bo'Nina (Banana Fofana Osama Bin Laden) Brown (Pierre Leverne Dease) challenges the definition of African-American queer identity and has brought to Atlanta an original perspective on the art of drag with her papercraft creations. Entering the workroom of Season 9 of *Drag Race* with one of the most original aesthetics, Nina showcased an epic slew of looks that ranged from skeleton hooker to Lady-Gaga-meets-working-girl fantasy to her jaw dropping Georgia peach which won her the first week's challenge. While her inner demons played with Nina's ability to get a foothold in the competition in the weeks to follow, she found herself winning lip-sync after lip-sync, demonstrating she has the performance chops to match the wild looks. After a stumble in the "Crew Better Work" makeover challenge, Nina Bo'Nina Brown sashayed away, promising to bring more of her epic makeover tutorials on YouTube to life and educate those queens back home in Atlanta that Nina's brand of drag SLAYS!

QUICK STATS

DRAG RACE: Season 9
RANKING: 6th place
SIGNATURE LOOK: Face Paint Fantasy Realness
TYPE: The Papercraft Queen
FAN-FAVOURITE PERFORMANCE: "Cola (Medley)" by Lana Del Rey

Nina Flowers

WHAT'S THE T?

Hailing from Bayamón, Puerto Rico, Jorge Flores Sanchez started doing drag at 19 against strong resistance from his family. Inspired by German punk rock artist Nina Hagen, Flores took her name and created Nina Flowers – an androgynous enigma that took the Denver drag scene by storm in 2008. Inherently creative like her Puerto Rican drag sisters back home, Flowers entered a drag scene populated by pageant queens and a pre-*Drag Race* world where the scene was not as established or welcoming as it is today.

Winning the online vote for the very first season of *RuPaul's Drag Race*, a then unknown TV competition loosely based on *America's Next Top Model*, Nina Flowers was from the outset a visually and conceptually different queen from pageant queens like Rebecca Glasscock, character impersonators like Shannel and dancing queens like Jade. Her honesty, warmth and heart were set against her strong and tattooed exterior making her such an original character that one could not only root for in the competition but adore her creativity and style. Finishing second to the first winner BeBe Zahara Benet, Nina took the title of Miss Congeniality and went back home to Denver where her drag was welcomed with open arms for the first time.

Following her appearances on *Drag Race* and *All Stars*, Nina has taken the club scene by storm. A star of the monthly Drag Nation in Denver, Nina continues to push boundaries with her style of Drag DJ'ing, releasing club singles and remixes, propelling her into the world of electronic music production. Nina is also lucky enough to have May 29 declared "Nina Flowers Day" in recognition of her contribution to Denver's LGBT community.

QUICK STATS

DRAG RACES:
Season 1 |
All Stars 1

RANKINGS:
2nd place (Miss Congeniality)
| 9th place

POST DRAG RACE:
Spins internationally as one of
the most in-demand circuit DJs;
released house singles including
"Loca" (2009) and "I'm Feelin'
Flowers" (2011); starred in the
music video for Adore Delano's
"I Look Fuckin' Cool"
with Alaska

SIGNATURE LOOK:
All Star Androgyny Realness

TYPE:
The Genderfuck Queen

**FAN-FAVOURITE
PERFORMANCE:**
"Addicted to Bass" by Puretone

"LOCAAAAAAAA!"

Drag term

MUG

A person's face. Queens considered strongest at "beating their mugs" include Raven, Miss Fame, Roxxxy Andrews, Milk and Raja.

Ongina

"My middle name is Ong and God didn't bless me with a certain 'ina'"

WHAT'S THE T?

LA-based queen with Filipino roots, Ongina (Ryan Ong Palao) was fascinated as a child with the American concept of Halloween and on her 21st birthday made her androgynous gender-bending debut in drag. Inspired by fashion and women's shoes, Ongina spent the next six years of her drag career building the bubbly personality and sharp style that was presented in the very first season of *Drag Race*. One of the original fan-favourites of the series, Ongina won both the Destiny's Child-flavoured "Girl Groups" challenge and the emotional "MAC Viva-Glam" challenge. Inspired by her own HIV diagnosis, which she tearfully revealed to the judges and the world, Ongina created an optimistic commercial for the MAC cosmetics line which won her the respect of audiences worldwide. After a stumble in the girl fighter makeover challenge Ongina was sent home packing by Bebe Zahara Benet in an electric lip-sync contest, but her pint-sized power and humility solidified her status as a legendary Racer. Since the *Race*, Ongina starred as one of the head professors on *RuPaul's Drag U* and continues to entertain in West California with her brand of high fashion, emotive drag performance.

QUICK STATS

DRAG RACE: Season 1
RANKING: 5th place
SIGNATURE LOOK: High Concept Couture Realness
TYPE: The Bald Beauty Queen
FAN-FAVOURITE PERFORMANCE: "Beautiful" by Christina Aguilera

"Anyone that's eaten my cherry pie raves about it."

QUICK STATS

DRAG RACES:
Season 2 | *All Stars* 1

RANKINGS:
2nd place (Miss Congeniality)
| 11th place

POST DRAG RACE:
Writes for the Gay Voices section of the *Huffington Post*; released pop singles including "Nice Car (Shame about Your Penis)" (2012) and "Different" (2014); starred in drag comedy series *She's Living for This* in 2013; hosts YouTube web series *The Pandora Boxx Show*

SIGNATURE LOOK:
Colourful Comedienne
Realness

TYPE:
The Susan Lucci of Drag

**FAN-FAVOURITE
PERFORMANCE:**
"Let It Go (Frozen Medley)",
by Various Artists

Pandora Boxx

WHAT'S THE T?

Inspired by fellow New York queen Darienne Lake, Pandora Boxx – the drag persona of Michael Steck – appeared on the Rochester drag scene in the mid-90s. Boxx, a classically styled female impersonator with a comedic flair, first appeared on US television screens in 1997 in an episode of *Ricki Lake* hilariously entitled "Get a grip doll... you're too fat to be a drag queen".

In 2009 Pandora Boxx was cast in the second season of *RuPaul's Drag Race*. Although her styling and aesthetic weren't to the taste of judge Santino Rice, Boxx won the hearts of fans through her camp schtick, killer impersonation of Carol Channing in the "Snatch Game" and through her honest discussion on suicide and depression. Crowned Miss Congeniality, Pandora went on to star in several spin-offs of *Drag Race* including *All Stars* and *Drag U*, as well as starring as the host of *Pandora Boxx's Drag Center* – a web series where Boxx would recap newly released *Drag Race* episodes.

Following her season on *Drag Race* Pandora became the first well-known comedy queen of the franchise and went on to star in stand up comedy specials, which have starred future contestant Bianca Del Rio and drag comedy legends Coco Peru and Jackie Beat. Pandora has joined other *Race* alumni in releasing pop singles including "Cooter!" (2014) and "Different" (2015). Still touring strongly with the Battle of the Seasons Tour as well as appearing on all of the Drag Race Cruises, Boxx maintains her status as one of the original fan-favourites bringing her brand of camp and comedy across the globe.

Drag term

KAIKAI

The act of sex between two drag queens. Often used to describe the act while both parties are dressed in drag, the term can also be used for drag queens hooking up out of drag as well. For example: "I know she's my sister but she's hot, so we decided to kaikai last night instead of finding trade".

Drag term

KIKI

"Kiki" is a term to describe gossip, small talk, chatting, or a heart-to-heart conversation and must *never* be confused with "kaikai"! As described by the Scissor Sisters, a "Kiki is a party for calming all nerves... sipping tea and dishing just deserts one may deserve". (See also: T/Tea/Tee.)

Pearl

WHAT'S THE T?

Originally from St Petersburg, Florida, Matthew James Lent began his drag career in Chicago as Pearl in 2012. A feast for the eyes, Pearl creates performances and high-fashion looks that meld both Hollywood glamour and electric club kid aesthetics. Although a fairly new queen on the scene, Pearl has been lucky enough to curate her own eccentric queer club nights *Pleasure* and *Pain for Pleasure*.

Pearl made her television debut on Season 7 of *RuPaul's Drag Race* in 2015. Executing intricately styled and aesthetically delicious looks on the main stage, Pearl was criticised for "falling asleep" throughout the competition. After the fire was lit under her by RuPaul for not making a splash like her fellow competitors, Pearl won two team-based main challenges with Max in a comedy hosting of the "DESPY Awards" and with Trixie Mattel as a "Conjoined Queen". Fighting off the early criticism, Pearl championed through to come as co-runner up with Ginger Minj.

Following *Drag Race* Pearl released her debut self-produced techno/dance album *Pleasure*, which featured the single "Love Slave" and charted at #11 on the US Billboard Dance/Electronic Album chart. In addition to releasing her own album, Pearl went on to team up with perfume company Xyrena to release "Flazéda", her very own signature fragrance.

"Bitch, I'm from
New York and
you can wear fur
in spring. 'K?"

QUICK STATS

DRAG RACE:
Season 7

RANKING:
Co-runner Up

POST DRAG RACE:
Produced and released her own
dance/techno album *Pleasure* in
2015; curated her own signature
fragrance "Flazéda"; starred
in the music video to Violet
Chachki's single "Bettie"

SIGNATURE LOOK:
Stepford Wife Robot Realness

TYPE:
The Old Hollywood Club Kid

**FAN-FAVOURITE
PERFORMANCE:**
"Hotride" by The Prodigy

Penny Tration

"Everybody likes a little Penny Tration."

WHAT'S THE T?

Inspired by the great Divine, Penny Tration (Tony Cody) started her career in drag over 20 years before her appearance on *Drag Race*, after encountering an entrancing performance by Louisville legend Hurricane Summers. An emcee extraordinaire and pageant winner with an fabulously old-school sense of wit and style, Penny was voted by the *Drag Race* Facebook fan community to be cast in Season 5 – and she was more than ready to bring her strong skillset to the competition. Presented with the challenge of dumpster diving for materials to create a unique piece of couture in the first challenge of the season, Penny was unable to put her fashion where her mouth was and was sent home in a purple gown (which she later resurrected in her live reunion club-kid inspired costume). Following her time on the *Race*, Penny Tration has continued to compete in pageants taking home the crown of Miss Ohio All American Goddess at Large 2014, and continuing to entertain crowds back home in Kentucky.

QUICK STATS

DRAG RACE: Season 5
RANKING: 14th place
SIGNATURE LOOK: Painted For The Gawds Realness
TYPE: The Effervescent Emcee Queen
FAN-FAVOURITE PERFORMANCE: "Carwash" by Rose Royce

Peppermint

"The number one queen is P-E-P-P-E-R-bitch, you know the rest!"

WHAT'S THE T?

New York drag royalty with one heck of a sweet tooth, Miss Peppermint (Agnes Moore) has been turning parties since the late 1990's as a live performance queen who serves equal doses of fabulous and fierce. As a triple-threat singer, songwriter and dancer, Peppermint has not only released minty fresh club jams with NYC icons Cazwell and Sherry Vine, but her legacy is built on her congeniality and passion for performance. Peppermint's bubbly personality won over her fellow Racers and fans alike on Season 9, while her witty work on the Michelle Visage roast showed she can do sticky just as well as sweet. Though a few pink ensembles in her early runways left audiences wanting more, her club kid couture stole the show and bolstered her journey to the crown. The undeniable lip-sync assassin of her season, Peppermint's explosive wins over Cynthia Lee Fontaine and Alexis Michelle whet the audience's appetite for her "Lip-sync For The Crown" at the finale. While placing second, Peppermint is more ready to take on the world with her brand of drag that isn't measured by gender or boundaries, simply by fierceness!

QUICK STATS

DRAG RACE: Season 9
RANKING: 2nd place
SIGNATURE LOOK: Candy Cane Club-kid Realness
TYPE: The NYC Legend
FAN-FAVOURITE PERFORMANCE: "Servin' It Up" by Peppermint feat. Cazwell

Phi Phi O'Hara

"At least I am a showgirl, bitch, go back to Party City where you belong."

WHAT'S THE T?

A fierce queen who is not only a killer performer, live singer and makeup artist but an inventive costume designer, Phi Phi O'Hara (Jaremi Carey) began her career as Lady Phoenix in 2004 prior to a move to Chicago and name change after joining the house of O'Hara under drag mother Asia O'Hara. A pageant winner prior to her time on Season 4, Phi Phi entered the competition with the crown in her sights and a fiery desire to win that caused conflict – her rivalry with winner Sharon Needles making for some epic gay TV! Winning the "Dragazine" and "DILF" makeover challenges, Phi Phi made the top three of the contest. Later cast in *All Stars* 2, O'Hara's efforts to "Rudeem" herself for Season 4's shady behaviour fell short after blow ups with Alyssa Edwards and a Twitter tirade against RuPaul. While her time on both seasons weren't the best of PR exercises for her brand, Phi Phi's immense talent hasn't been completely out-shadowed, as her *365 Days of Drag* Instagram project in 2016 solidified her status as an iconic queen of cosplay, not the "tired-ass showgirl" from years ago.

QUICK STATS

DRAG RACE: Season 4 | *All Stars* 2
RANKING: Co-runner Up | 7th place
SIGNATURE LOOK: Cosplay Chameleon Realness
TYPE: The Showgirl-turned-Cosplay Queen
FAN-FAVOURITE PERFORMANCE: "Anything You Can Do I Can Do Better Medley" by Various

Phoenix

"I can play well with others... But, I definitely do have a bitchy side!"

WHAT'S THE T?

A seasoned artist serving equally high glam and edgy androgynous looks, Phoenix (Brian Trapp) from Atlanta is also the drag daughter of the legendary Nicole Paige Brooks. In the ten years of drag before appearing on the third season of *Drag Race*, Phoenix not only showcased her show production and dance ability on stages across the South but she is a formidable costume designer, inspired by pop culture and designers like Alexander McQueen and Thierry Mugler. Though only lasting two episodes in her season, losing a Lady Gaga "Bad Romance" lip-sync challenge to Delta Work following the "Queens In Space" challenge, Phoenix used her experience on *Drag Race* to continue the evolution of her persona, changing her aesthetic and elevating her artistry to the high standard she presents today. With a strong sense of community in mind, Phoenix continues to perform across the South and now works as one of the top nightclub entertainment directors in Atlanta.

QUICK STATS

DRAG RACE: Season 3
RANKING: 12th place
SIGNATURE LOOK: Lusciousness in a Leotard Realness
TYPE: The Fiery Club Queen
FAN-FAVOURITE PERFORMANCE: "Fancy" by Reba McEntire & Iggy Azalea

"Victoria is very outgoing ...
she likes to meet men..."

QUICK STATS

DRAG RACE:
Season 1

RANKING:
9th place

POST DRAG RACE:
Featured as part of the Miley
Cyrus performance of "Dooo It!"
at the 2015 MTV Video Music
Awards; continues entertaining
crowds with the *Dreamgirls
Revue* alongside *Drag Race*
alumni Shannel and Morgan
McMichaels; featured in an
episode of *RuPaul Drives*

SIGNATURE LOOK:
Miss America Pageant Realness

TYPE:
The Old School Showgirl

**FAN-FAVOURITE
PERFORMANCE:**
"EOY (Entertainer Of The Year)
2010 Performance" from *Dreamgirls
(Original Soundtrack)*

Porkchop

WHAT'S THE T?

Beginning her drag career in 1987, Victoria "Porkchop" Parker was created from the mind of North Carolina's Victor Bowling. An astute and well-seasoned pageant queen, Porkchop has participated in over 200 pageants, won over 100 and taken four national titles including Miss Continental Plus in 2003. Inspired by Elizabeth Taylor, Porkchop's aesthetic is classic pageant drag, which has served her well for over two decades. Porkchop has starred in two documentaries on the pageantry system; *Trantasia* (2006) a documentary on The World's Most Beautiful Transexual Pageant and *Pageant* (2008) as a lead cast member vying for the title of Miss Gay America.

Cast in the first season of *RuPaul's Drag Race*, Porkchop holds the title of the first queen eliminated from the entire show, and as a result receives a warm welcome from RuPaul herself at all of the live reunion shows. Although an already polished and expert drag performer, it was Porkchop's weak sewing skills that brought about her early dismissal in the first challenge. Porkchop gave a show-stopping performance of RuPaul's "Supermodel" against Akashia in the first ever Lip-sync for Your Life of the series.

Porkchop has relentlessly toured since Season 1 concluded in 2009 and was lucky enough to be featured on stage with over 30 other drag queens at the 2015 MTV Video Music Awards for the Miley Cyrus performance. She is currently a member of Chad Michaels' *Dreamgirls Revue* based in California.

The Princess

"Putting on the makeup, the wig, the costume... unleashes her!"

WHAT'S THE T?

A queen who isn't afraid of flipping a wig and serving bald beauty is Chicago's The Princess (Adam Biga), who delivers a mash-up of avant garde and couture, eclectic and posh drag. Born in Johannesburg, South Africa, and self taught in makeup, styling and dressmaking since the age of 18, The Princess's first ever audition saw her cast in Season 4 where she found herself among other edgy and atypical queens like Sharon Needles. However after two low performances in the "Glamazons vs. Champions" commercial and "Wrestling's Trashiest Fighters" challenges and two lip-syncs for her life, The Princess was eliminated much earlier in the competition than what was expected for a queen with her experience. Evolving her aesthetic to challenge the boundaries of drag, The Princess continues to serve up looks for days on her Instagram, performs regularly in Nashville and has been a fan-favourite at RuPaul's Drag Con convention in recent years.

QUICK STATS

DRAG RACE: Season 4
RANKING: 11th place
SIGNATURE LOOK: Andro Eclecticism Realness
TYPE: The Punk Princess
FAN-FAVOURITE PERFORMANCE: "Welcome To The Black Parade"
by My Chemical Romance

Drag term

READING

An advanced format of the insult, "Reading" is the art of criticising by wittily and incisively exposing a person's flaws (i.e. "to *read* them like a book"). On *RuPaul's Drag Race*, queens are invited to participate in "The Library" (referring to the act of one reading a book in a library), a mini challenge in which contestants are invited to read their fellow queens "to filth" (to thoroughly insult or to call attention to flaws).

Raja

WHAT'S THE T?

LA's Sutan Amrull has performed as Raja Gemini for over 20 years as a self-described "glitter hippie, artist, performer, model and muse". Having dropped out of university, Raja decided early on that she had a flair for the artistic – painting, drawing and makeup artistry. Raja started drag in the early 1990s house music club scene where she created thrift store outfits and joined other punk club queens in the LA night life. Inspired by Leigh Bowery and rebelling against the sequins and shoulder pads, the edgy Raja was born and began not only her drag career but started working as a makeup artist. This artistry has formed the basis of Raja's career, which has seen her not only tour with Adam Lambert as his principal makeup artist, but saw her serve as makeup artist for nine cycles of Tyra Banks' *America's Next Top Model*.

Competing in *RuPaul's Drag Race* was a walk in the park for the likes of Raja – a seasoned performer with incomparable wit and sewing skills. Winning three main challenges and stealing the scene at every runway in looks ranging from African Zulu Realness to Rainbow Brite Cosplay, Raja easily took the crown beating fellow "Heather" Manila Luzon and Alexis Mateo in the final episode.

In the years following her win, Raja has released her own offbeat and edgy music videos and singles including the Latino pop "Cholita" (2015) and Bollywood electro-disco "Zubi Zubi Zubi" (2013). Raja also now stars in the weekly web series *Fashion Photo RuView* with Raven with whom she was also a Drag Professor on the spin-off show *RuPaul's Drag U*.

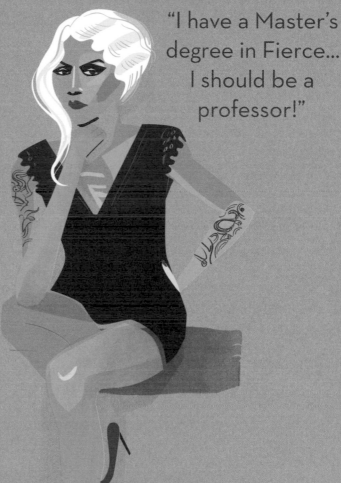

"I have a Master's degree in Fierce... I should be a professor!"

QUICK STATS

DRAG RACE:
Season 3

RANKING:
Winner

POST DRAG RACE:
Toured the US as Iggy Azalea's principal makeup artist; co-host of World of Wonder's *Fashion Photo RuView* with Raven; released singles "Diamond Crowned Queen" (2011), "Zubi Zubi Zubi" (2013) and "Cholita" (2015)

SIGNATURE LOOK:
Around The World In 80 Days Realness

TYPE:
The Drag Chameleon

FAN-FAVOURITE PERFORMANCE:
"In My Arms" by Kylie Minogue

When
you become the
image of your
IMAGINATION,
it's the most powerful
thing you could
ever do

DRAG RACES:
Season 2 | *All Stars* 1

RANKINGS:
2nd place | 2nd place

POST DRAG RACE:
Co-host of World of Wonder's
Fashion Photo RuView; music
video pin-up (MNDR's "Feed
Me Diamonds"); star of *RuPaul's
Drag Race* spin-offs *Drag U* and
Drag My Dinner with Jujubee
and Manila Luzon

SIGNATURE LOOK:
Dark Temptress Realness

TYPE:
The Stone Cold Vixen

**FAN-FAVOURITE
PERFORMANCE:**
"Megacolon" by Fischerspooner

"I'm a man
in a dress – I'm a
psychological
woman."

Raven

WHAT'S THE T?

After a stint as a male go-go dancer by the name of Phoenix, David Petruschin from Riverside, California took flight and and emerged as Raven in the West Hollywood drag scene in 2002. Raven started her drag career alongside legendary sisters Morgan McMichaels and Mayhem Miller performing shows that suited her taste for the underground – stylish and electronic. A fan of non-mainstream artists like Fischerspooner, Róisín Murphy and Miss Kittin, Raven's performance style separated her from the pack as a dark horse.

Raven appeared on the second season of *RuPaul's Drag Race* and soon became a fan-favourite for her quick wit, icy yet fierce composure and striking aesthetic. Raven's style was equally matched with her makeup artistry, which saw her execute so many varied looks from baby blue blushing bride to *Cabaret*-era Liza and country sweetheart realness to disco-diva-meets-accomplished-author. Although incredibly determined and styled to the gods, Raven was pipped at the post by both Tyra Sanchez in Season 2 and Chad Michaels in the first season of *All Stars*.

Following the *Race*, Raven co-hosts the weekly web series *Fashion Photo RuView* with Season 3 winner Raja, summoning her expert style, hair and makeup knowledge to "toot and boot" the looks of new *Drag Race* contestants on the runway. Commencing with Season 9 of *Drag Race*, Raven was appointed as a Creative Producer and makeup artist for RuPaul herself, beating the mug of mother for the gawds while fellow racer Delta Work commands the Supermodel of the World's weaves!

Rebecca Glasscock

"If I'm so horrible and such a bitch, why would I give you my brand new green contacts?"

WHAT'S THE T?

Fort Lauderdale's Rebecca Glasscock (Javier Rivera), who found her drag surname in a gay men's dating magazine, appeared on Season 1 after performing for several years in her local bar scene under the guidance of drag mother Misty Eyez. The OG fish, Rebecca made her entrance into the workroom serving girl-next-door realness contrasting with some of the more outlandish and body-revealing looks presented by her castmates. A favourite of the judges for her realness, a reserved Rebecca often found herself in hot water with her fellow contestants who would cite the favouritism when it came to Rebecca's makeover main challenge win and subsequent top three placing. While not often performing alongside her *Race* sisters outside of reunion gigs, Glasscock continues to perform in local Florida bars and has been pursuing an acting career, successfully landing a cameo as an alien drag queen in *Men In Black 3*.

QUICK STATS

DRAG RACE: Season 1
RANKING: 3rd place
SIGNATURE LOOK: High School Sweetheart Realness
TYPE: The Original Fish
FAN-FAVOURITE PERFORMANCE: "Show Me How You Burlesque"
by Christina Aguilera

Robbie Turner

"Am I the first girl that has ever broken a light on the runway?"

WHAT'S THE T?

After a one-off stint as a Liza Minnelli in 2005, Seattle's Robbie Turner (Jeremy Baird) caught the drag bug and began her career as a full-time performer impersonating the likes of Lady Gaga and Kylie Minogue before morphing into the old-Hollywood queen audiences saw on Season 8. Ready to serve impressive period looks that channel the starlets of 1930's–60's cinema, Robbie entered the *Race* with big shoes to fill as previous Seattle contestants Jinkx Monsoon and BenDeLaCreme revealed how important being well-read on history and artistry is to drag performers from that city. Though Robbie found herself on roller skates lip-syncing for her life early in the contest, she channelled her inner Deborah Harry in the "New Wave Queens" challenge, taking the win in front of Blondie herself! While she has a keen eye for period fashion, it was her costume construction skills in the "Wizards of Drag" challenge that cut Robbie's time on *Drag Race* short. Since then, Turner has focussed her time into writing *I'll Tell You For Free*, a book and solo show that tells the "tales, follies and inconceivable truths from the life of a drag queen".

QUICK STATS

DRAG RACE: Season 8
RANKING: 7th place
SIGNATURE LOOK: Vintage Vixen Realness
TYPE: The Classic Cinema Queen
FAN-FAVOURITE PERFORMANCE: "The Name Game" by Jessica Lange

Roxxxy Andrews

WHAT'S THE T?

At 21 Michael Feliciano from Orlando made his first appearance in drag at a Halloween celebration and soon became the pageant beauty Roxxxy Andrews. Her namesake a fusion of *Chicago*'s Roxie Hart and her drag mother, the legendary Erica Andrews, Roxxxy was inspired by the Orlando drag pageant. Drag sister of Detox, who also hails from Orlando, Roxxxy had taken numerous pageantry titles in her formative years including Miss West Virginia Continental Plus 2008 and 2009, the prestigious Miss Continental Plus 2010 and Miss West Virginia Continental 2012.

In 2013 Roxxxy Andrews was cast in *RuPaul's Drag Race* alongside drag sisters Detox and Alaska with whom the clique "Rolaskatox" was formed. A formidable contestant throughout, Roxxxy won the first costuming challenge as well as the "Super Troopers" makeover challenge. In an iconic Lip-sync for Your Life performance Roxxxy executed a wig reveal to Willow Smith's "Whip My Hair" that floored judges RuPaul and Michelle Visage who admitted, "I think I peed a little bit. Serious!". Finishing as a co-runner up with fan-favourite Alaska, Roxxxy Andrews fought heavy criticism from the public for her perceived bullying of winner Jinkx Monsoon.

Following *Drag Race* Roxxxy took on the role as principal makeup artist for Tamar Braxton (whom she impersonated in the "Snatch Game") on her US tour and walked the Marco Marco runway in 2014. Returning to serve sickening looks on the *All Stars* 2 runway, Roxxxy Andrews' journey to fourth place may have been the result of "Rolaskatox" voting strategies but she managed to "Ru-deem" herself with audiences with a new humble attitude towards the competition.

"I'm Roxxxy Andrews and I'm here to make it clear..."

QUICK STATS

DRAG RACE:
Season 5 | *All Stars 2*

RANKING:
Co-runner Up | 4th place

POST DRAG RACE:
Toured as Tamar Braxton's principal makeup artist; competed in 2015 Miss Southernmost USofA Pageant (1st Runner Up); Featured on RuPaul's single "Read U Wrote U" (2016)

SIGNATURE LOOK:
Pageant Perfection Realness

TYPE:
The Thick 'N' Juicy Queen

FAN-FAVOURITE PERFORMANCE:
"Talent Medley (at Miss Southernmost USofA 2015)" by Various Artists

Sahara Davenport

"Competition is on bitches!"

WHAT'S THE T?

A queen from NYC that always aimed to entertain the kids, school the girls and spread fierceness throughout the land, Sahara Davenport (Antoine Ashley) was not only a shining star of the city's drag scene but was also the partner of *Drag Race* sister Manila Luzon. While living in Dallas as a college student, Sahara started her career utilising her classical training in dance to get a foothold in the world of drag artistry before being cast in Season 2 in 2010. Winner of the "Starrbootylicious" challenge demonstrating her charisma, uniqueness, nerve and talent with a stripper pole, Sahara went on to pirouette her way through a lip-sync contest against Morgan McMichaels and rock it out in the "Rocker Chicks" challenges before being eliminated. After the *Race*, Sahara was one of the first ever Racers to release her own dance singles ("Go Off" and "Pump With Me" are bonafide pop jams)! Sadly in 2012, Sahara Davenport passed away from heart failure. Her legacy lays in the humility of her persona and her fierce attitude that will be remembered by *Drag Race* fans for years to come as the series' "eternal queen".

QUICK STATS

DRAG RACE: Season 2
RANKING: 7th place
SIGNATURE LOOK: Runway Fish Realness
TYPE: The Ballet School Beauty Queen
FAN-FAVOURITE PERFORMANCE: "Medley" by Whitney Houston

Sasha Belle

"I feel like I have cracked the code."

WHAT'S THE T?

A former Miss Gay Iowa who presides over her own hometown drag contest series for newcomers, Sasha Belle (Jared Breakenridge) is a young drag mother that got her start in 2006. A self-proclaimed *Drag Race* scholar and mega fan, Sasha's sixth audition for the *Race* was her golden ticket into the cast of Season 7 where she brought her mash-up of camp glamour and club-ready chameleon to the cut. After a not-quite-nude illusion in the first week's challenge, Sasha found herself among the bottom queens before being eliminated the following week after a forgettable performance in the "Glamazonian Airways" challenge and an unrealised "jet set eleganza" runway presentation. While her time on *Drag Race* didn't live up to Sasha Belle's expectations, she has continued to value her time on the show while show directing and producing *Sasha Belle's Drag Race* back home in Iowa.

QUICK STATS

DRAG RACE: Season 7
RANKING: 13th place
SIGNATURE LOOK: Gun-slingin' Glam Realness
TYPE: The Drag Mom of Iowa
FAN-FAVOURITE PERFORMANCE: "Crazy In Love (2014 Remix)" by Beyoncé

Sasha Velour

"Gender is a construct – tear it apart!"

WHAT'S THE T?

Inspired by gender expression, visual artistry and queer history, it was through study abroad in Russia that Sasha Velour (Sasha Steinberg) built on what had been a lifetime of playing with dress-up to curate a drag persona and aesthetic that encapsulates the spirit of icons like Leigh Bowery and Grace Jones. Sasha's trademark bald head is not only a tribute to her late mother who battled cancer, but speaks to her desire to challenge generic drag clichés and craft a new definition for drag beauty. Entering the Season 9 workroom with a scream, Sasha delivered high fashion, high colour and intelligent takes on the challenges each week, with two maxi challenge wins alongside Shea Couleé in the "Good Morning Bitches" and TV pilot challenges. A true runway panther, Sasha Velour delivered epic eleganza, with her "Gayest Ball Ever" creations and makeover looks pushing her through to the finale where after two theatre-shaking Whitney Houston lip-sync battles she won the ninth *Drag Race* crown.

In what has become the year of Sasha Velour, she not only took the title of America's Next Drag Superstar, but was awarded Drag Queen of the Year as well as Best Visual Artist at the 5th Annual Brooklyn Nightlife Awards in 2017.

QUICK STATS

DRAG RACE: Season 9
RANKING: Winner
SIGNATURE LOOK: Graphic Brow Realness
TYPE: The Wearable Art Queen
FAN-FAVOURITE PERFORMANCE: "This Woman's Work" by Kate Bush

Serena ChaCha

"This is the best quinceañera present ever!"

WHAT'S THE T?

A fine arts student from Panama with a keen interest in surrealism as well as soft sculpture and its relationship with the artistry of drag, Serena ChaCha (Myron Morgan) built her drag persona for three years before her appearance on Season 5 of *Drag Race*. Serving super-sweet-sixteen realness on her arrival in the workroom, the sweetness turned sour with her castmates backstage in the *Untucked* lounge after a poor performance in the "Lip-sync Extravaganza Eleganza" and some sideways comments about how her education plays a role in her drag artistry. In one of the most famous scenes of *Untucked*, Serena found herself ambushed by almost the entire cast of Season 5 after calling other queens "ghetto" and "uneducated" before a lip-sync against Monica Beverly Hillz to Rihanna's "Only Girl". While her time on the *Race* was short and explosive, Serena ChaCha's career following has focussed on elevating her brand of Latina glamazon drag while building her own custom wig empire as both a stylist and savvy businesswoman!

QUICK STATS

DRAG RACE: Season 5
RANKING: 13th place
SIGNATURE LOOK: Miss Panama Realness
TYPE: The Educated Queen
FAN-FAVOURITE PERFORMANCE: "Grown Woman" by Beyoncé

"Halleloo!"

QUICK STATS

DRAG RACES:
Season 2 | Season 3

RANKINGS:
12th place | 5th place

POST DRAG RACE:
Starred on *Dance Moms* in 2011
as a guest mentor teaching her
signature Death Drop; performed
"Let's Have a Kiki" by Scissor
Sisters on *Glee* alongside Sarah
Jessica Parker (2012); released
dance single "Werqin' Gurl"
(2012)

SIGNATURE LOOK:
Post-modern-pimp-ho Realness

TYPE:
The Sickening Southern Belle

**FAN-FAVOURITE
PERFORMANCE:**
"Turn Me Out" by Kathy Brown

Shangela

WHAT'S THE T?

A comedian from Paris, Texas, DJ Pierce – better known as Shangela Laquifa Wadley – started performing drag professionally in 2009. She was only five months into her career in the LA drag scene before being cast in the second season of *RuPaul's Drag Race*. A member of the Haus of Edwards, Shangela cites *Drag Race* alumni Alyssa Edwards as her drag mother.

Although being eliminated first in Season 2 and subsequently winning the Entertainer of the Year 2010 pageant in Los Angeles, Shangela was re-cast in the third season of *Drag Race* where she finished in fifth place after a strong performance throughout the season. Shining in her characterisation of "Laquifa – the post-modern-pimp-ho" in the "Ru Ha Ha" comedy challenge, it was evident that while sewing wasn't necessarily her strong point, Shangela is one hell of a performer. The character of Laquifa went on to star on stage in her own comedy show as well as on *One Night Stand Up* on Logo TV. A fan-favourite *Drag Race* moment, Shangela's "out of the box" appearance in Season 3 was spoofed in Season 4 when Shangela announced she was cast in that competition.

A "werqin' gurl" through and through, Shangela has continued to deliver stand up comedy sets, including the Bianca Del Rio Roast for her 40th birthday. Teaming up with Lady Gaga and Courtney Act, the dancing diva starred in the lyric video of Gaga's "Applause" filmed at the famous Micky's in West Hollywood. Shangela has also been a busy queen on screen with appearances in TV shows *Dance Moms*, *Glee*, *2 Broke Girls* and *The Mentalist*.

Drag term

REALNESS

"Realness" can be used to describe the act of appearing feminine, but the term can also follow a noun to describe the act of appearing to be a convincing realistic, authentic, or accurate version of said noun. For example: "Bebe Zahara Benet was serving jungle queen realness!" (Bebe's presentation was amazing; I believed she was truly a queen of the jungle.)

Shannel

"I am amazed at myself..."

WHAT'S THE T?

A drag legend with roots in both Las Vegas and California, more than two decades of mastery of the art of female impersonation and the first body queen of *Drag Race*, Shannel (Bryan Watkins) is a diva for all seasons. An unparalleled (ex-Chanel) makeup artist with the ability to transform into countless different characters, Shannel appeared on the first season of *Drag Race* with not only the body but the charisma, uniqueness, nerve and talent to take out the crown. While Shannel's confidence often came off as her playing the grande dame, her aesthetic execution was always impeccable and her devotion to her artistry never wavered. Her iconic Medusa lip-sync to Whitney Houston's "The Greatest Love of All" and the "I am beautiful" moment before the judges bolstered her status as a legendary queen of the *Race*. She was soon cast in the first season of *All Stars*, where she won three main challenges in a row with Chad Michaels. Following her time on Season 1, Shannel was a professor on *Drag U*, as well as working on hair and makeup behind the scenes. In recent years, she has moved back to Las Vegas where she is one of the most in-demand queens on The Strip starring in *Frank Marino's Divas*.

QUICK STATS

DRAG RACE: Season 1 | *All Stars* 1
RANKING: 4th place | 4th place
SIGNATURE LOOK: 39 Character Illusions Realness
TYPE: The Original Body Queen
FAN-FAVOURITE PERFORMANCE: "My Immortal" by Evanescence

Sharon Needles

WHAT'S THE T?

Originally from Iowa, Sharon Needles moved to Pittsburgh in 2004 where she began working as a drag performer in nightclubs and later with the legendary experimental troupe the Haus of Haunt, which Needles described as "one punk rock, messy mash up of very talented, fucked up weirdos". It was here that Aaron Coady became the legendary Sharon Needles of today. The Pittsburgh collective included fellow *Drag Race* alumni, and later partner, Alaska, who shone through the season after Needles' debut.

In 2012 Needles appeared on the fourth season of *Drag Race* and quickly gained a dedicated fan base dying for her ghoulish, original style – in a season heavy with fishy, fashion-focused queens. Less an underdog than someone completely ignored among the breast-plates and sparkles, Needles repeatedly performed well – winning four of the challenges and only having to lip-sync for her life once (where she battled it out with on-screen nemesis Phi Phi O'Hara). In the close-run finale, Needles snatched the crown from Chad Michaels to become The Next Drag Superstar.

Since *Drag Race*, Needles has busied herself releasing two self-funded albums *PG-13* (2013) and *Taxidermy* (2015). Sharon Needles has also become the face of PETA and regularly hosts horror and suspense B-movies on Logo TV. Sharon continues to tour her live act as a part of the Battle of the Seasons tour alongside *Drag Race* alumni Ivy Winters, Detox and Phi Phi O'Hara.

"I'm a stupid genius, reviled sweetheart and PBR princess."

QUICK STATS

DRAG RACE:
Season 4

RANKING:
Winner

POST DRAG RACE:
Released debut album *PG-13* (2013) featuring singles "This Club Is a Haunted House" and "I Wish I Were Amanda Lepore"; spokesperson for People for the Ethical Treatment of Animals (PETA); was honoured by the Pittsburgh City Council declaring 12 June 2012 the official "Sharon Needles Day"

SIGNATURE LOOK:
Undead Goth Gurl Realness

TYPE:
The B-movie Beauty

FAN-FAVOURITE PERFORMANCE:
"Sweet Transvestite" from *The Rocky Horror Picture Show (Original Soundtrack)*

Shea Couleé

"I didn't come to play, I came to slay."

WHAT'S THE T?

A queen with a background in costume design and a doctorate in FIERCE, Chicago's Shea Couleé (Jaren Merrell) has served equal parts boujee and bourgie since her 2012 start in local drag competition *Roscoe's Drag Race*. Following the footsteps of her fellow windy city sisters Pearl and Kim Chi, Shea appeared on Season 9 of *Drag Race* entering the work room, furry armed and leotarded, determined to nab the crown. Stealing the show as Blac Chyna in the musical challenge, snatching back-to-back team wins with Sasha Velour in the pilot and talk show challenges and then gloriously taking home the win for the "Gayest Ball Ever", Shea Couleé executed one of the best runs in *Drag Race* herstory all the while stomping the runway like a pro ("why y'all acting brand new?"). In one of the season's biggest shocks, Shea found herself lip-syncing for the crown against new sister Sasha to Whitney Houston's "So Emotional" and was ultimately pipped at the post. Determined to slay regardless, Shea Couleé's debut EP *Couleé-d* and its music video anthology dropped as Season 9 wound-up to a close, giving fans a healthy dose of Beyoncé's *Lemonade* teas with a fierce serve of Couleé brilliance!

QUICK STATS

DRAG RACE: Season 9
RANKING: 3rd place/4th place
SIGNATURE LOOK: Leotarded Lemonade Realness
TYPE: The All-rounder Queen
FAN-FAVOURITE PERFORMANCE: "Partition" by Beyoncé

Sonique

"My mom sent me to a military school in hopes that she'd get a little soldier. Needless to say she got a drag queen!"

WHAT'S THE T?

A small-town showgirl who worked the Atlanta scene alongside local legends Angelica D'Paige and Shawna Brooks, Sonique (Kylie Sonique Love) began her drag career at landmark club Blakes on the Park. Sauntering into Season 2, this Georgia peach brought her Southern charm and backflips to the main stage as she fought for the crown before a gutting post-"Snatch Game" elimination against new friend Morgan McMichaels. Sonique revealed in the Reunion that she had been in the process of transitioning, which was held off during the audition and filming of the show. In living her truth after her season, the ever-fierce Sonique moved to LA, has walked the runway with Marco Marco and continues entertaining week-in-week-out on the Southern California scene as part of showcasts at Micky's and the *Dreamgirls Revue*.

QUICK STATS

DRAG RACE: Season 2
RANKING: 9th place
SIGNATURE LOOK: Buxom Bombshell Realness
TYPE: The Backflip Belle of the South
FAN-FAVOURITE PERFORMANCE: "Love Hangover/Heartbreaker"
by Mariah Carey

Stacy Layne Matthews

"Henny!"

WHAT'S THE T?

The undisputed breakout star of Season 3, Stacy Layne Matthews – or Queen Henny as her fans have dubbed her – from Back Swamp, North Carolina, had been performing in drag and participating in pageants for almost nine years before being cast in Season 3 of *Drag Race*. A small-town queen with the biggest heart of her season, Stacy (Stacy Jones) entered the race with skills as a theatre buff and gifted singer, with her acting chops nabbing her a win in the "Snatch Game" as Mo'Nique. Unfortunately, it was Stacy's seamstress abilities that saw her serve a not-so-sweet red velvet cake couture creation in the "Face Face Face of Cakes" challenge which landed her in RuPaul's firing line. Since the *Race*, the popularity of her memes have kept audiences laughing with Stacy Layne Matthews while her gender-identity realisation has allowed her to blossom on a personal level, enabling newfound confidence as she continues to perform in drag and produce in 2017 her first NYC cabaret show *From Stacy, With Love...*

QUICK STATS

DRAG RACE: Season 3
RANKING: 8th place
SIGNATURE LOOK: Curvy Country Glam Realness
TYPE: The Back Swamp Beauty Queen
FAN-FAVOURITE PERFORMANCE: "Diamonds (Live)" by Rihanna

Drag term

SERVE

To present oneself in a particular way to the best of your ability and, in the context of drag performance, giving the audience what they want. Inspired by a queen's runway presentation you could say something like: "Detox was serving some *Fifth Element* realness on the runway last night – she gave me life!".

QUICK STATS

DRAG RACES:
Season 1 | *All Stars* 1

RANKINGS:
8th place | 10th place

POST DRAG RACE:
Released albums *Hot Skunkx* (2014), *Discos Undead* (2010) and *Popcorn* (2009); member of the band Rollz Royces with *Drag Race* alumni Kelly Mantle and long-time collaborator Michael Catti; starred in an advertisement for travel company Orbitz with fellow *All Stars* alumni Raven, Manila Luzon and Latrice Royale

SIGNATURE LOOK:
Yesteryear Glam Realness

TYPE:
The Countess of Kooky

FAN-FAVOURITE PERFORMANCE:
"What's Love Got to Do With It" by Tina Turner

"I don't see you out there walking children in nature."

Tammie Brown

WHAT'S THE T?

A drag icon of the Southern Californian scene, Tammie Brown – the creation of Keith Glen Schubert – got her start doing drag as a teenager in theatre productions of *Grease* and *Into the Woods*. Inspired by Tina Turner and Dustin Hoffman's *Tootsie*, Brown delivers an original blend of drag that recalls old Hollywood with an eccentric twist. Prior to her appearance on *Drag Race*, Tammie appeared on *The Surreal Life* and *How Clean Is Your House?*, and auditioned unsuccessfully for *America's Got Talent*.

Joining the first cast of *RuPaul's Drag Race*, Tammie was already one to stand out from the pack of nine queens vying for the title of the first ever America's Next Drag Superstar. Although her appearance lasted two episodes, Tammie – in true Brown fashion – vowed not to lip-sync for her life to Michelle Williams' "We Break the Dawn" against Akashia and simply smiled and danced back and forth into elimination. An iconic appearance at the Season 1 Reunion saw Brown go head to head with RuPaul and the judges on the merits of her drag and bullying from the judges – neither Ru nor Tammie were having a bar of it! The all-round zaniness of Tammie Brown won her a spot in the first season of *All Stars* where we were all "teleported to Mars".

After her Drag Race stints, Tammie Brown has continued to release offbeat folk and pop music including singles "Whatever", "Clam Happy", "Love Piñata" and "Walking Children in Nature" with long-time collaborator Michael Catti. On the social justice front, our #QueenWithACause has continued her famous educational nature walks with city youth and has advocated to Free The Orcas from Seaworld in the United States. Tammie Brown's inspirational imagination just hasn't stopped, as she had begun selling in 2016 her own unique handmade dolls – Rag Queenz – online and at RuPaul's Drag Con.

Tatianna

"Thank you."

WHAT'S THE T?

A queen who had started playing with drag as early as 14 years old, Tatianna (Joey Santolini) entered Season 2 having only *performed* in drag a handful of times. Often judged by the other queens in her season as inexperienced, relying on her looks or simply being a judge's favourite, Tatianna fought tooth and nail to prove that she deserved to compete for the title of America's Next Drag Superstar, winning the "Snatch Game" as Britney Spears and delivering consistent performances in the main challenges. It was Tatianna's fierceness in the face of dismissive competitors and immense growth after the show that lead to her casting in the second season of *All Stars*, where the beauty queen of Virginia was given a chance to prove her star quality to a modern *Drag Race* audience. Slaying the talent show with her spoken word performance "The Same Parts", audiences saw Tati with their hands turning it out week after week culminating in an epic Rihanna lip-sync against Alyssa Edwards demanding a double "shantay you stay". A bonafide fan-favourite now, Tatianna has been able to tour across Europe and Australia, release dance singles and rock the MTV Video Music Awards red carpet in full Aaliyah impersonation drag!

QUICK STATS

DRAG RACE: Season 2 | *All Stars* 2
RANKING: 4th place | 6th place
SIGNATURE LOOK: Teen Queen Superstar Realness
TYPE: The Femme Fatale
FAN-FAVOURITE PERFORMANCE: "The Same Parts" by Tatianna

Tempest DuJour

"Who's ready for some hot tuna casserole? 'Cause mama's home."

WHAT'S THE T?

Arizona university professor Tempest DuJour (Patrick Holt) had only started doing drag ten years before appearing on the seventh season of *Drag Race*, citing a love for the Shakespearean theatre and camp aesthetics. Having been one of the go-to stock photography queens for years, the immediately recognisable face of drag, Mama Tempest (she's got two!) appeared on *Drag Race* popping out her own offspring in a hilarious workroom entrance. After a heated squabble about being an older queen with competitor Kandy Ho, this delicate flower of the desert found herself lip-syncing to RuPaul's "Geronimo" against Kandy after a crabby nude illusion runway presentation. Eliminated first from her cut of queens, Tempest DuJour has been described as one of the strongest "first out" from the entire series and has continued entertaining fans with her live shows, WOW Presents featured videos and her starring role in the 2017 drag queen comedy film *Cherry Pop* alongside Racers Bob The Drag Queen and Detox.

QUICK STATS

DRAG RACE: Season 7
RANKING: 14th place
SIGNATURE LOOK: Colourful Campy Realness
TYPE: The Drag Professor
FAN-FAVOURITE PERFORMANCE: "Defying Gravity" from *Wicked*

If you can't love yourself how the hell are you gonna love somebody else?

Drag term

SICKENING

To be beyond awesome, incredibly amazing, or particularly attractive in appearance or performance. Alexis Mateo from Season 3 famously told us that being a drag queen in the United States was not only "BAM!" but that she is "Sickening! No?".

Thorgy Thor

"Witty catchphrase, you know what I mean?"

WHAT'S THE T?

An alternative drag performance artist that got her start performing drag characters in theatre shows, Thorgy Thor (Shane Thor Galligan) worked the New York and Brooklyn scenes for over 12 years prior to appearing on *Drag Race* – including winning the LEGEND Award at the 2014 Brooklyn Nightlife Awards. An accomplished violinist inspired by NYC icon Joey Arias, Thorgy auditioned for every season of *Drag Race* before Ru decided that Thorgy had relaxed and was ready for Season 8. A consistently safe queen in the challenges, Thorgy delivered colourfully chic runway presentations that were complemented by her superbly smart performances in the "Snatch Game" as Michael Jackson and in her writing of the "Street Meatz" New Wave parody. The unfortunate victim of Chi Chi DeVayne's drag assassination in the "Black and White" runway lip-sync to "And I Am Telling You I'm Not Going", Thorgy left the competition far earlier than many fans had hoped. Following her time on Season 8, Thorgy has ensured her local NYC fans receive their regular dose of her Thorgeousness, while her eighty-piece orchestra show ("Thorchestra") is still in the works.

QUICK STATS

DRAG RACE: Season 8
RANKING: 6th place
SIGNATURE LOOK: Fashion Clown Realness
TYPE: The Dreadlocks Darling
FAN-FAVOURITE PERFORMANCE: "Philip Seymour Hoffman" by Thorgy Thor

Trinity K. Bonet

"The 'K' is for Kardashian but we don't use that for legal reasons."

WHAT'S THE T?

A pageant queen with an exceptionally supportive stage mother to keep her showgirl in check, Trinity K. Bonet (Joshua Jamal Jones) is another queen who had her start in drag after a Halloween performance at a family party. Inspired to make her sick mother proud by auditioning, Trinity took her expansive drag collection into Season 6 with eyes on the prize and sense of old school drag skill and performance that represented her roots in both Miami and Atlanta. Straight out of the gate Trinity demonstrated masterful costume construction and makeup artistry with her party supplies inspired Queen Amidala meets geisha look, which continued throughout the *Race* with show stopping costumes. It was Trinity's initial closed-off nature that found the brunt of cast mate Bianca Del Rio's criticism, however after an empowering sharing of her HIV story and a personal breakthrough with her own competition goals, Trinity soared and won over the judges and fans alike. Eliminated after a stumble in the "Drag Queens of Talk" interview challenge, Trinity has focussed her energy after *Drag Race* into curating her impeccable Beyoncé impersonation act and snatching pageant crowns including Miss Sweetheart International 2015.

QUICK STATS

DRAG RACE: Season 6
RANKING: 7th place
SIGNATURE LOOK: Sasha Fierce Realness
TYPE: The Young Glamazon
FAN-FAVOURITE PERFORMANCE: "Formation" by Beyoncé

Trinity Taylor

"I call shade!"

WHAT'S THE T?

The bad-ass beauty with a Kardashian booty, Trinity "The Tuck" Taylor (Ryan Taylor) is an Alabama-born queen who got her start in Orlando, Florida. An entertainer who effortlessly teeters the lines of high glamour and working girl, Trinity is the ultimate pageant queen who not only has the drag girl parody down – check out La'Whore's "Shlong" – but was crowned with the highest pageant honour of Entertainer of the Year in 2014, beating out *Drag Race* alum Alyssa Edwards (who placed runner-up). Easily the queen to beat from the outset, Trinity delivered a *Drag Race* run that was not only full of straight-up gag for her inimitable tuck, but demonstrated growth while she had audiences laughing all the way to the finale with her shelarious winning performances in the "9021-HO" and "Draggily Ever After" challenges. Having turned-out ass-out iconic Taylor looks all season – and even snatching a win for her makeover of crew member Rizzo – Trinity's final four presentation was a pageant fan's dream while her lip-sync performance against Peppermint, while not successful, kept audiences cheering on the Trin-Train. Winning over so many new fans with her irreverence and charm while maintaining the integrity of pageant drag in *Drag Race*, Trinity Taylor is now not only an Entertainer of the Year, but a world class legend of the *Race* – *All Stars* 3, anyone?

QUICK STATS

DRAG RACE: Season 9
RANKING: 3rd place/4th place
SIGNATURE LOOK: Silicone Siren Realness
TYPE: The Master Mother Tucker
FAN-FAVOURITE PERFORMANCE: "Titanium/Bionic" by Sia & Christina Aguilera

Trixie Mattel

WHAT'S THE T?

Brian Firkus of Milwaukee, Wisconsin, began his drag career as Trixie Mattel, rebelling against the rough relationship he had with his stepfather – her namesake a reclaimed slur that Mattel would suffer at his hands. Though she won her first and only pageant there, Trixie was cut from a different yarn to many pageant queens, so a move to Chicago made for a fresh career challenge. It was here that she began working with Chicago club icon Kim Chi (who later appeared on Season 8) and perfected her now legendary overdrawn Barbie-inspired mug and curated the comedic drag act fans across the world have grown to love.

Cast in Season 7 of *Drag Race*, Trixie Mattel was an instant favourite for not only her original look but for her quick wit. Although shining in the "Glamazonian Airways" challenge, Trixie soon faced criticism for not standing out from the pack in her team's parody "Tan With U" and lost her Lip-sync for Your Life against Pearl. Following heavy criticism on social media for eliminating Trixie, RuPaul brought back all of the eliminated contestants in the "Conjoined Queens" challenge to earn a spot back in the competition. Teaming up with Pearl again as debutant twins, Trixie – the less-pretty twin – won her way back in the competition for another two episodes demonstrating both comedic and costuming skills that were lacking in earlier episodes.

Although she didn't make the top three, Mattel's star has continued to rise along with her fanbase numbers as a result of not only her viral YouTube series *UNHhhh* with Katya, but her debut country/folk record *Two Birds* which crossed over to the mainstream reaching #5 on the UK Country and #2 on the US Heatseekers (new artist) charts. With a hit-record under her belt and over 650,000 followers on Instagram awaiting her next moves, Trixie Mattel is one to watch as her brand of plastic fantastic fantasy drag takes over!

QUICK STATS

DRAG RACE:
Season 7

RANKING:
6th place

POST DRAG RACE:
Guest starred on *American Horror Story: Roanoke* as herself; hosts WOW Presents web series *UNHhhh* alongside Season 7 sister Katya; performed her live material across the United States with the 2017 Dragapalooza Live Tour

SIGNATURE LOOK:
Life-in-plastic Realness

TYPE:
The Life-size Doll

FAN-FAVOURITE PERFORMANCE:
"Barbie Girl" by Aqua

"I'm like the knock-knock joke of drag."

Drag term

SQUIRREL
FRIENDS

A term used to describe a girlfriend who,
just like a squirrel, hides her nuts.

Drag term

TUCK

The act of a drag queen pulling back his genitals using duct tape or tight underwear to create the illusion of having a flat and feminine crotch area. A "meaty tuck" (as described by RuPaul about Season 1's Jade) is a poorly executed tuck, which is large, lumpy or bulging.

"I'm not a bitch – I'm America's sweetheart."

QUICK STATS

DRAG RACE & RANKING:
Season 2 | Winner

POST DRAG RACE:
Became the subject of documentary film *Drag Dad* about her role as both a drag queen and father; starred as a fierce Drag Professor on *RuPaul's Drag U*; appeared as a Kim Zolciak doppelgänger on an episode of *The Real Housewives of Atlanta*

SIGNATURE LOOK:
Red Carpet Beyoncé Realness

TYPE:
The Seasoned Ingénue

FAN-FAVOURITE PERFORMANCE:
"Drunk in Love" by Beyoncé

Tyra Sanchez

WHAT'S THE T?

Florida's James Ross IV began his drag career after leaving high school at 16. Raised by her drag mother who brought her out of homelessness, Tyra Sanchez was taught in the trade of old-school Florida pageant drag and began impersonating Beyoncé in shows across the Orlando gay scene.

Looking to challenge herself and bring about a new life for her young son Jeremiah, Tyra was cast in the second season of *RuPaul's Drag Race*. Despite her youth, Tyra demonstrated a wide array of drag tricks and sickening stage looks. Winning three main challenges, Sanchez brought out her comedic side in the "Country Queens" challenge and was complimented by RuPaul for her old-school drag conduct in the "Here Comes the Bride" runway. Tyra's off-stage bridezilla drama with Tatianna provided iconic *Untucked* moments bringing the supplementary show to the forefront in its early inception. Never having to lip-sync for her life, Tyra Sanchez took the crown in a photo finish against Raven in a performance of RuPaul's "Jealous of My Boogie".

The youngest contestant to ever take the title of America's Next Drag Superstar, Tyra Sanchez went on to release her first single "Look at Me" in 2011 and work on a Kickstarter-funded feature documentary by Björn Flóki called *Drag Dad*. Since taking the crown Tyra has been considered M.I.A. from the *Drag Race* spotlight, which she revealed in a 2015 episode of web series *Hey Qween* was the result of her focusing on being the caretaker parent for her son Jeremiah in the formative years of his schooling.

Valentina

"Hello it's me – Valentina!"

WHAT'S THE T?

A young queen with a refreshing take on classic drag performance and style, Valentina (James Leyva) famously performed live in drag venues for only ten months before appearing on the ninth season of *Drag Race*. A well researched queen of unparalleled beauty and poise, Valentina served not only looks that complemented her Mexican heritage but she also brought humility and kindness to the show with the aim of showing that a Latin queen doesn't need to be the butt of jokes, but a role model. After a stumble in the TV pilot challenge with Nina Bo'Nina Brown, Valentina found herself eliminated in the first ever lip-sync for your life where RuPaul stopped the contest demanding Valentina to take an obstructing mask away from her mouth. Valentina admitted that while the competition got the better of her and she wasn't prepared for the lip-sync, she is ready to show the world that the fierceness she demonstrated up until that point will help propel her career as the future face of Latin American drag!

QUICK STATS

DRAG RACE: Season 9
RANKING: 7th place (Miss Congeniality)
SIGNATURE LOOK: Telenovela Glamour Realness
TYPE: The Chicana Goddess
FAN-FAVOURITE PERFORMANCE: "Asi Fue" by Isabel Pantoja

Venus D-Lite

"I don't think you can be the Next
Drag Superstar with no confidence."

WHAT'S THE T?

With the title of being the only male Madonna impersonator in a major
motion picture – *The Comebacks* (2007) – Los Angeles' Venus D-Lite (Adam
Guerra) is one of the world's premier impersonators of the Queen of Pop and
has enjoyed a successful full-time career as a drag queen since studying at
film school. A regular on the West Hollywood scene like many Racers from
Season 3 of *Drag Race*, Venus was only able to entertain audiences with her
brash yet colourful persona for one episode after a blunder in the "Queens
Who Mopped Christmas" costume challenge that resulted in a wig-flipping
messy lip-sync against Shangela. Since appearing on *Drag Race*, Venus D-Lite
has not only kept her Madonna impersonation act at the top of booking
agent's charts, but she has appeared on reality shows *My Strange Addiction*
and *Botched*. Venus can also be found in the *Ripley's Believe It Or Not!
Annual*, which cites her expensive obsession with emulating the Material Girl
– racking up more than $175,000 in plastic surgery fees!

QUICK STATS

DRAG RACE: Season 3
RANKING: 13th place
SIGNATURE LOOK: "Who's That Girl" Realness
TYPE: The Iconic Impersonator
FAN-FAVOURITE PERFORMANCE: "Dress You Up" by Madonna

Violet Chachki

WHAT'S THE T?

Starting her career using a fake ID to gain entry into local Atlanta drag shows, Violet Chachki (Jason Dardo) was taken under the wing of drag mother Dax Exclamationpoint (who later appeared on Season 8 of *Drag Race*) and soon became a regular cast member at nightclub Jungle. Working alongside Amanda Lepore and drag royalty Lady Bunny, Violet quickly cut her teeth and learned not only how to beat her face for the gods but learned burlesque show tricks like waist cinching and aerial silk performance. Chachki came into early notoriety for being photographed in the possession of Sharon Needles' official winner's crown after it was stolen during a 2012 gig in Atlanta – Chachki was later found innocent of the theft.

In 2015 Chachki was cast in *Drag Race* serving week after week of unmatchable runway looks. Winning the first main challenge, despite criticism from Michelle Visage for her un-cinched "boy body", Violet Chachki went on to win three main costume-based challenges. An expert in design and costume execution, her "I really could die bitch" 18-inch waist runway presentation floored the judges and fellow competitors. Chachki never fell into the bottom two and took the crown from Ginger Minj and Pearl in the live taped reunion finale. Much like young winner Tyra Sanchez, Chachki received heavy criticism for her cold and bitchy yet determined performance throughout the season.

Following her win on *Drag Race* Chachki has released her debut EP *Gagged* and attended the 2015 MTV Video Music Awards as Miley Cyrus' red carpet partner and on-stage dancer in the performance of "Dooo It!".

> "Pain is beauty and I'm the prettiest."

QUICK STATS

DRAG RACE:
Season 7

RANKING:
Winner

POST DRAG RACE:
Released debut EP *Gagged* (2015) featuring single "Bettie" starring Pearl in the music video; performs "The Night Before Christmas" on the Christmas album *Christmas Queens* (2015); represented *RuPaul's Drag Race* at New York Fashion Week appearances with Miss Fame

SIGNATURE LOOK:
Dita Von Teese Pin-up Realness

TYPE:
The Burlesque Bondage Beauty

FAN-FAVOURITE PERFORMANCE:
"Million Dollar Man" by Lana Del Rey

Vivacious

"Mother has arrived!"

WHAT'S THE T?

Vivacious (Osmond Vacious) – one of the original 1990's NYC club kids – has spent more than two decades creating an intergalactic drag explosion of colour, futurism and pop art as a performer and DJ. Having worked predominantly in the straight nightclub scene in New York, Vivacious' "living art" aims to bridge the gap between the gay and straight communities – her appearance on Season 6 providing her an opportunity to school the children across the world. Entering the work room stalled by a zipper malfunction revealing a lit-up glittered head named Ornacia, Vivacious' offbeat character and quotable catchphrases won audiences immediately, even though her costume construction and "Scream Queens" acting efforts didn't inspire the judges. After two lip-syncs against Kelly Mantle and April Carrión, Vivacious and Ornacia were sent on their way back to NYC leaving a newer understanding of yesteryear's club kid style that inspired its own runway challenge in Season 9. Since appearing on *Drag Race* Vivacious has appeared in several WOW Presents webisodes, performed on MTV with Miley Cyrus and joined Katy Perry on stage on Saturday Night Live in 2017 vogueing and cracking her fans, keeping the club kid vibe alive!

QUICK STATS

DRAG RACE: Season 6
RANKING: 13th place
SIGNATURE LOOK: 90's Club Kid Realness
TYPE: The Legendary Neon Queen
FAN-FAVOURITE PERFORMANCE: "Twisted" by Peter Rauhofer

Vivienne Pinay

"I will always be the fishiest queen today, tomorrow, next month, the past seasons, and the next seasons to come."

WHAT'S THE T?

Having created her drag persona watching *RuPaul's Drag Race* since its inception, New York's Vivienne Pinay (Michael Donehoo) had been working in the beauty industry for almost a decade before competing for the crown in Season 5. A goddess with Filipino heritage and an unclockable Nicki Minaj impersonation act, Vivi came, slayed and conquered as far as her runway presentations and makeup transformations were concerned. After a lacklustre lip-sync to Britney Spears' "Oops I Did It Again", Vivienne and Honey Mahogany found themselves ousted in the first ever double-elimination of the series. Maintaining a friendship with Alyssa Edwards after Season 5, Pinay not only worked on-set as a personal assistant and makeup artist on the *Alyssa's Secret* web series, but she was made an honorary member of the House of Edwards, appearing in her own spin-offs of the series impersonating her new drag mother.

QUICK STATS

DRAG RACE: Season 5
RANKING: 10th/11th place
SIGNATURE LOOK: Goddess Glam Realness
TYPE: The Fierce Filipina Fish
FAN-FAVOURITE PERFORMANCE: "Minaj Medley" by Nicki Minaj

"I'm not gonna RuPaulogize for anything that I'm doing now."

DRAG RACE & RANKING:
Season 4 | 7th place

POST DRAG RACE:
Performed as a member of viral drag troupe DWV as well as with the AAA Girls; released solo albums *The Wreckoning* (2012) and *Shartistry In Motion* (2015); starred in TV's *The New Normal* (2013) and *CSI* (2012) and the film *Kicking Zombie Ass for Jesus* (2013); produces YouTube series The *Beatdown* and *Paint Me Bitch*

SIGNATURE LOOK:
Whore Clown Realness

TYPE:
The Model, Actress, Mattress, Whorespondent, Ice Cream Man

FAN-FAVOURITE PERFORMANCE:
"Rich Girl" by Hall and Oates

Willam

WHAT'S THE T?

Willam Belli's drag career began somewhat simultaneously with her acting career in the early 2000's with appearances on *The District*, *Boston Public* and her starring role on *Nip/Tuck* as a transgender woman, Cherry Peck. Supplementing her acting career with live performance, Willam formed the band Tranzkuntinental with fellow drag queens Detox, Vicky Vox, Kelly Mantle and Rhea Litré in 2009 before releasing her own solo parody "The Vagina Song" in 2012.

Cast in the fourth season of *RuPaul's Drag Race*, Willam was from the outset an accomplished screen queen with killer comedy chops to boot – a rule-breaker with impeccable style. Never forgetting to name-drop a co-star, designer shoe or ex-*Sex and the City* worn Dolce and Gabbana coat, Willam presented realness on the main stage and slayed the competition winning the "Float Your Boat" main challenge. Although a fan-favourite, Willam's time on *Drag Race* was short lived after a series of rules were broken in the now famous "What Did Willam Do?" shock elimination.

Willam can be credited as one of the hardest working *Drag Race* alumni with the release of two full-length solo albums and over 20 singles (including her girl group foray with Alaska and Courtney Act as the AAA Girls), her shelarious web content like "*The Beatdown*" and *Paint Me Bitch*, which has garnerned more than 140 million views on her YouTube channel, as well as her first ever book – *Suck Less: Where There's A Willam There's A Way* – paving the glitter-smudged pathway for queens to follow for years to come.

Yara Sofia

"Echa pa'lante."

WHAT'S THE T?

Commanding the arts of makeup, costume design, hair manipulation and, of course, drag, Puerto Rico's Yara Sofia (Gabriel Burgos Ortiz) was inspired by the dark Finnish-American actress Maila Nurmi and the designs of Alexander McQueen to create a persona that was equally sweet and evil. One of the standouts of Season 3 of *RuPaul's Drag Race*, Yara Sofia took gothic drag to the mainstream with countless original presentations on the main stage, earning her the respect of queens for her uniqueness and talent but also the public who crowned her Miss Congeniality of the season. Her unparalleled hair artistry gave her a main challenge win, which lead to her casting in the first season of *All Stars* – where she brought her classic Latina charm and humour to win the "RuPaul's Gaff-In" challenge with Team Yarlexis partner Alexis Mateo. In the years after her appearance on *All Stars*, Yara has walked Marco Marco runways, performed across the world and has moved to Las Vegas where she is now one of the key queens on The Strip, bringing her brand of hyper-glam-Latina-goth-fantasy to the fans of Sin City.

QUICK STATS

DRAG RACE: Season 3 | *All Stars* 1
RANKING: 4th place (Miss Congeniality) | 5th place
SIGNATURE LOOK: Gothic Latina Realness
TYPE: The Dark-Sided Queen
FAN-FAVOURITE PERFORMANCE: "Work Your Body/Echa pa'lante" by Thalia

Drag term

WERK

To do something with a large amount of fiery attitude, vitality and vigour with the intent to impress and stun. "Werk" can also be used as an exclamation of approval: "You better werk bitch!" – RuPaul.

LIPS

YNC

SEASON ONE

	CONTESTANTS	SONG	ELIMINATED
1	Akashia vs. Victoria "Porkchop" Parker	"Supermodel (You Better Work)" by RuPaul	Victoria "Porkchop" Parker
2	Akashia vs. Tammie Brown	"We Break the Dawn" by Michelle Williams	Tammie Brown
3	Akashia vs. Shannel	"The Greatest Love of All" by Whitney Houston	Akashia
4	Jade vs. Rebecca Glasscock	"Would I Lie to You" by Eurythmics	Jade
5	BeBe Zahara Benet vs. Ongina	"Stronger" by Britney Spears	Ongina
6	Rebecca Glasscock vs. Shannel	"Shackles" by Mary Mary	Shannel
7	BeBe Zahara Benet vs. Nina Flowers	"Covergirl (Put The Bass In Your Walk)" by RuPaul	Nina Flowers

SEASON TWO

	CONTESTANTS	SONG	ELIMINATED
1	Sahara Davenport vs. Shangela	"Covergirl (Put The Bass In Your Walk)" by RuPaul	Shangela
2	Nicole Paige Brooks vs. Raven	"My Lovin' (You're Never Gonna Get It)" by En Vogue	Nicole Paige Brooks
3	Mystique Summers Madison vs. Raven	"I Hear You Knocking" by Wynonna Judd	Mystique Summers Madison
4	Morgan McMichaels vs. Sonique	"Two Of Hearts" by Stacey Q	Sonique
5	Morgan McMichaels vs. Sahara Davenport	"Carry On" by Martha Wash	Morgan McMichaels
6	Jujubee vs. Sahara Davenport	"Black Velvet" by Alannah Myles	Sahara Davenport
7	Jessica Wild vs. Tatianna	"He's The Greatest Dancer" by Sister Sledge	Jessica Wild
8	Jujubee vs. Pandora Boxx	"Shake Your Love" by Debbie Gibson	Pandora Boxx
9	Jujubee vs. Tatianna	"Something He Can Feel" by Aretha Franklin	Tatianna
10	Raven vs. Tyra Sanchez	"Jealous Of My Boogie" by RuPaul	Raven

SEASON THREE

	CONTESTANTS	SONG	ELIMINATED
1	Venus D-Lite vs. Shangela	"The Right Stuff" by Vanessa Williams	Venus D-Lite
2	Delta Work vs. Phoenix	"Bad Romance" by Lady Gaga	Phoenix
3	India Ferrah vs. Mimi Imfurst	"Don't Leave Me This Way" by Thelma Houston	Mimi Imfurst
4	India Ferrah vs. Stacy Layne Matthews	"Meeting In The Ladies Room" by Klymaxx	India Ferrah
5	Delta Work vs. Mariah	"Looking For A New Love" by Jody Watley	Mariah
6	Alexis Mateo vs. Stacy Layne Matthews	"Knock On Wood" by Amii Stewart	Stacy Layne Matthews
7	Delta Work vs. Manila Luzon	"Macarthur Park" by Donna Summer	Delta Work
8	Carmen Carrera vs. Yara Sofia	"Mickey" (Spanish version) by Toni Basil	*No elimination*
9	Carmen Carrera vs. Shangela	"Believe" by Cher	Carmen Carrera
10	Alexis Mateo vs. Shangela	"Even Angels" by Fantasia	Shangela
11	Carmen Carrera vs. Raja	"Straight Up" by Paula Abdul	Carmen Carrera
12	Alexis Mateo vs. Yara Sofia	"I Think About You" by Patti Labelle	Yara Sofia
13	Manila Luzon vs. Raja	"Champion" by RuPaul	Manila Luzon

SEASON FOUR

	CONTESTANTS	SONG	ELIMINATED
1	Alisa Summers vs. Jiggly Caliente	"Toxic" by Britney Spears	Alisa Summers
2	Lashauwn Beyond vs. The Princess	"Bad Girls" by Donna Summer	Lashauwn Beyond
3	Dida Ritz vs. The Princess	"This Will Be (An Everlasting Love)" by Natalie Cole	The Princess
4	Madame LaQueer vs. Milan	"Trouble" by Pink	Madame LaQueer
5	Kenya Michaels vs. Milan	"Vogue" by Madonna	Kenya Michaels
6	Jiggle Caliente vs. Milan	"Born This Way" by Lady Gaga	Milan
7	Jiggle Caliente vs. Willam	"Mi Vida Loca (My Crazy Life)" by Pam Tillis	Jiggle Caliente
8	Phi Phi O'Hara vs. Sharon Needles	"It's Raining Men (The Sequel)" by Martha Wash and RuPaul	*No elimination; Willam disqualified*
9	Dida Ritz vs. Latrice Royale	"I've Got To Use My Imagination" by Gladys Knight	Dida Ritz
10	Kenya Michaels vs. Latrice Royale	"(You Make Me Feel Like) A Natural Woman" by Aretha Franklin	Kenya Michaels
11	Chad Michaels vs. Latrice Royale	"No One Else On Earth" by Wynonna Judd	Latrice Royale
12	Chad Michaels vs. Phi Phi O'Hara vs. Sharon Needles	"Glamazon" by RuPaul	*No elimination*

SEASON FIVE

	CONTESTANTS	SONG	ELIMINATED
1	Penny Traition vs. Serena Chacha	"Party In The U.S.A." by Miley Cyrus	Penny Traition
2	Monica Beverly Hillz vs Serena Chacha	"Only Girl (In The World)" by Rihanna	Serena Chacha
3	Coco Montrese vs. Monica Beverly Hillz	"When I Grow Up" by The Pussycat Dolls	Monica Beverly Hillz
4	Honey Mahogany vs. Vivienne Pinay	"Oops!... I Did It Again" by Britney Spears	*Double elimination*
5	Detox vs. Lineysha Sparx	"Take Me Home" by Cher	Lineysha Sparx
6	Coco Montrese vs. Jade Jolie	"I'm So Excited" by The Pointer Sisters	Jade Jolie
7	Alyssa Edwards vs. Roxxxy Andrews	"Whip My Hair" by Willow Smith	*No elimination*
8	Alyssa Edwards vs. Ivy Winters	"Ain't Nothin' Goin' On But The Rent" by Gwen Guthrie	Ivy Winters
9	Alyssa Edwards vs. Coco Montrese	"Cold Hearted" by Paula Abdul	Alyssa Edwards
10	Coco Montrese vs. Detox	"(It Takes) Two To Make It Right" by Seduction	Coco Montrese
11	Detox vs. Jinkx Monsoon	"Malambo No.1" by Yma Sumac	Detox
12	Alaska vs. Jinkx Monsoon vs. Roxxxy Andrews	"The Beginning" by RuPaul	*No elimination*

SEASON SIX

	CONTESTANTS	SONG	ELIMINATED
1	Kelly Mantle vs. Vivacious	"Express Yourself" by Madonna	Kelly Mantle
2	Darienne Lake vs. Magnolia Crawford	"Turn The Beat Around" by Vicki Sue Robinson	Magnolia Crawford
3	April Carrión vs. Vivacious	"Shake It Up" by Selena Gomez	Vivacious
4	April Carrión vs. Trinity K Bonet	"I'm Every Woman" by Chaka Khan	April Carrión
5	Gia Gunn vs. Laganja Estranja	"Head To Toe" by Lisa Lisa & Cult Jam	Gia Gunn
6	Milk vs. Trinity K Bonet	"Whatta Man" by Salt-N-Pepa with En Vogue	Milk
7	Bendelacreme vs. Darienne Lake	"Point Of No Return" by Exposé	*No elimination*
8	Joslyn Fox vs. Laganja Estranja	"Stupid Girls" by Pink	Laganja Estranja
9	Adore Delano vs. Trinity K Bonet	"Vibeology" by Paula Abdul	Trinity K Bonet
10	Adore Delano vs. Joslyn Fox	"Think" by Aretha Franklin	Joslyn Fox
11	Bendelacreme vs. Darienne Lake	"Stronger (What Doesn't Kill You)" by Kelly Clarkson	Bendelacreme
12	Adore Delano vs. Bianca Del Rio vs. Courtney Act vs. Darienne Lake	"Sissy That Walk" by RuPaul	Darienne Lake

SEASON SEVEN

	CONTESTANTS	SONG	ELIMINATED
1	Kandy Ho vs. Tempest DuJour	"Geronimo" by RuPaul	Tempest DuJour
2	Katya vs. Sasha Belle	"Twist Of Fate" by Olivia Newton-John	Sasha Belle
3	Jasmine Masters vs. Kennedy Davenport	"I Was Gonna Cancel" by Kylie Minogue	Jasmine Masters
4	Pearl vs. Trixie Mattel	"Dreaming" by Blondie	Trixie Mattel
5	Kandy Ho vs. Mrs Kasha Davis	"Lovergirl" by Teena Marie	Mrs Kasha Davis
6	Jaidynn Diore Fierce vs. Kandy Ho	"Break Free" by Ariana Grande	Kandy Ho
7	Jaidynn Diore Fierce vs. Max	"No More Lies" by Michel'le	Max
8	Ginger Minj w/ Sasha Belle vs. Jaidynn Diore Fierce w/ Tempest DuJour	"I Think We're Alone Now" by Tiffany	Jaidynn Diore Fierce
9	Miss Fame vs. Pearl	"Really Don't Care" by Demi Lovato	Miss Fame
10	Ginger Minj vs. Trixie Mattel	"Show Me Love" by Robin S	Trixie Mattel
11	Katya vs. Kennedy Davenport	"Roar" by Katy Perry	Katya
12	Ginger Minj vs. Kennedy Davenport vs. Pearl vs. Violet Chachki	"Born Naked" by RuPaul	Kennedy Davenport

SEASON EIGHT

	CONTESTANTS	SONG	ELIMINATED
1	Laila McQueen vs. Naysha Lopez	"Applause" by Lady Gaga	Naysha Lopez
2	Dax Exclamationpoint vs. Laila McQueen	"I Will Survive" by Gloria Gaynor	*Double elimination*
3	Cynthia Lee Fontaine vs. Robbie Turner	"Mesmerized (Freemasons Radio Edit)" by Faith Evans	Cynthia Lee Fontaine
4	Chi Chi DeVayne vs. Naysha Lopez	"Call Me" by Blondie	Naysha Lopez
5	Acid Betty vs. Naomi Smalls	"Causing A Commotion" by Madonna	Acid Betty
6	Derrick Barry vs. Robbie Turner	"I Love It" by Icona Pop ft. Charli XCX	Robbie Turner
7	Chi Chi DeVayne vs. Thorgy Thor	"I'm Telling You I'm Not Going" by Jennifer Holliday	Thorgy Thor
8	Bob The Drag Queen vs. Derrick Barry	"You Make Me Feel (Mighty Real)" by Sylvester	Derrick Barry
9	Bob The Drag Queen vs. Chi Chi DeVayne vs. Kim Chi vs. Naomi Smalls	"The Realness" by RuPaul	Chi Chi DeVayne

SEASON NINE

	CONTESTANTS	SONG	ELIMINATED
1	Jaymes Mansfield vs. Kimora Blac	"Love Shack" by The B-52's	Jaymes Mansfield
2	Aja vs. Kimora Blac	"Holding Out For A Hero" by Bonnie Tyler	Kimora Blac
3	Charlie Hides vs. Trinity Taylor	"I Wanna Go" by Britney Spears	Charlie Hides
4	Cynthia Lee Fontaine vs. Farrah Moan	"Woman Up" by Meghan Trainor	*No elimination; Eureka removed*
5	Cynthia Lee Fontaine vs. Peppermint	"Music" by Madonna	Cynthia Lee Fontaine
6	Aja vs. Nina Bo'Nina Brown	"Finally" by CeCe Peniston	Aja
7	Alexis Michelle vs. Farrah Moan	"Baby I'm Burnin'" by Dolly Parton	Farrah Moan
8	Nina Bo'Nina Brown vs. Valentina	"Greedy" by Ariana Grande	Valentina
9	Nina Bo'Nina Brown vs. Shea Coulee	"Cool for the Summer" by Demi Lovato	Nina Bo'Nina Brown
10	Alexis Michelle vs. Peppermint	"Macho Man" by Village People	Alexis Michelle
11	Peppermint vs. Sasha Velour vs. Shea Couleé vs. Trinity Taylor	"U Wear It Well" by RuPaul	*No elimination*
12A	Peppermint vs. Trinity Taylor	"Stronger" by Britney Spears	Trinity Taylor
12B	Sasha Velour vs. Shea Couleé	"So Emotional" by Whitney Houston	Shea Couleé
13	Peppermint vs. Sasha Velour	"It's Not Right But It's Okay" by Whitney Houston	Peppermint

Hey Porkchop!

ALL STARS SEASON ONE

	CONTESTANTS	SONG	ELIMINATED
1	Chad Michaels vs. Mimi Imfurst	"Opposites Attract" by Paula Abdul	Team Mandora (Mimi Imfurst & Pandora Boxx)
2	Latrice Royale vs. Tammie Brown	"There's No Business Like Show Business" by Ethel Merman	Team Brown Flowers (Nina Flowers & Tammie Brown)
3	Jujubee vs. Manila Luzon	"Nasty" by Janet Jackson	Team Latrila (Latrice Royale & Manila Luzon)
4	Alexis Mateo and Yara Sofia vs. Raven	"Don't Cha" by The Pussycat Dolls	Team Yarlexis (Alexis Mateo & Yara Sofia)
5	Jujubee vs. Raven	"Dancing On My Own" by Robyn	*No elimination*
6	Chad Michaels vs. Raven	"Responsitrannity" by RuPaul	Raven

ALL STARS SEASON TWO: LIP-SYNC FOR YOUR LEGACY

	CONTESTANTS	SONG	ELIMINATED
1	Roxxxy Andrews vs. Tatianna	"Shake It Off" by Taylor Swift	Roxxxy Andrews eliminated Coco Montrese
2	Alaska vs. Katya	"Le Freak (Freak Out)" by Chic	Alaska eliminated Tatianna
3	Alyssa Edwards vs. Detox	"Tell It To My Heart" by Taylor Dayne	Alyssa Edwards eliminated Ginger Minj
4	Alaska vs. Phi Phi O'Hara	"Got To Be Real" by Cheryl Lynn	Alaska eliminated Alyssa Edwards
5	Alyssa Edwards vs. Tatianna	"Shut Up & Drive" by Rihanna	Alyssa Edwards & Tatianna eliminated Phi Phi O'Hara
6	Alaska vs. Katya	"Cherry Bomb" by Joan Jett & The Blackhearts	Alaska eliminated Tatianna
7	Detox vs. Katya	"Step It Up" by RuPaul ft. Dave Aude	Detox eliminated Alyssa Edwards
8	Alaska vs. Detox vs. Katya	"If I Were Your Woman" by Gladys Knight & The Pips	Detox & Katya eliminated

Published in 2017 by Smith Street Books
Melbourne | Australia
smithstreetbooks.com

ISBN: 978-1-925418-57-6

CIP data is available from the National Library of Australia.

Publisher: Paul McNally
Design concept: Kate Barraclough
Design layout: Heather Menzies
Writer: John Davis
Illustrator: Libby VanderPloeg

Printed & bound in China by C&C Offset Printing Co., Ltd.

Book 45
10 9 8 7 6 5 4 3

Sashay.